Civil War Atlanta

I0809475

Civil War
Atlanta

Robert Scott Davis

The History Press

Published by The History Press
Charleston, SC 29403
www.historypress.net

Copyright © 2011 by Robert S. Davis

All rights reserved

Cover image: 1888 lithograph of the Battle of Atlanta by Lois Kurz and Alexander Allison.

First published 2011

Manufactured in the United States

ISBN 978.1.59629.763.0

Library of Congress Cataloging-in-Publication Data

Davis, Robert Scott, 1954-
Civil War Atlanta / Robert S. Davis.
p. cm.
Includes bibliographical references and index.
ISBN 978-1-59629-763-0
1. Atlanta (Ga.)--History, Military--19th century. 2. Georgia--History--Civil War, 1861-1865. 3. Atlanta Campaign, 1864. 4. Atlanta (Ga.)--History--19th century. I. Title.
F294.A857D28 2011
973.7'371--dc22
2010052979

Notice: The information in this book is true and complete to the best of our knowledge. It is offered without guarantee on the part of the author or The History Press. The author and The History Press disclaim all liability in connection with the use of this book.

All rights reserved. No part of this book may be reproduced or transmitted in any form whatsoever without prior written permission from the publisher except in the case of brief quotations embodied in critical articles and reviews.

In memory of Franklin Garrett, Atlanta's great friend and historian.

And in memory of the
Atlanta Historical Bulletin, Atlanta Historical Journal *and* Atlanta History,
three remarkable journals of scholarship that have now themselves become history.

There is HISTORY that is based on hard, documented fact; history that is colored with rumor, speculation, or falsehood; and history that exists in what might be termed the hinterlands of the imagination.
—*S.C. Gwynne,* Empire of the Summer Moon

Contents

Introduction

We now approach the sesquicentennial of the American Civil War. I grew up in the Atlanta area during its centennial (and my grandchildren, when my age, will see the bicentennial). During those years, I looked forward to my school's annual sack-lunch field trips to Kennesaw Mountain National Battlefield Park and to the cyclorama painting of the Battle of Atlanta in Grant Park. Family outings took me to see Stone Mountain Park and, at that time, abandoned beginnings of the Confederate memorial carved on its face, even before the creation of the modern park and its train pulled by a reproduction of either the General or the Texas of Great Locomotive Chase fame. As a boy, I had a copy of the print used on the cover of this book. I refought the Battles of Atlanta, Chickamauga and Kennesaw Mountain over and over again with my toy soldiers, complete with national cemeteries and battlefield monuments.

Those places would make real the lore, however factually wrong, of my family's role in the war. Today, my mother shares with her great-grandchildren memories of her great-grandfather, a veteran of Robert E. Lee's army and one of the last Confederate veterans, who died when she was eight.

Dizzying as these circumstances seem, I feel like I have been writing this book most of my conscious life. Despite my earlier research on Atlanta projects like *Requiem for a Lost City*, I have learned much and had great fun doing this new work. Uncovering the story of Civil War Atlanta, if one does not want to just rehash everyone else's books, requires special friends such as the late Franklin M. Garrett and Colonel James G. Bogle, as well as aid from such experts as Gail Miller DeLoach, print archivist of the Georgia Archives, and Ken Denney. Mr. Denney has done intensive documentary research to combine the Civil War photographs of Atlanta in such a way as to re-create the city of 1864. David M. Sherman, Dr. Keith Bohannon, Paul Graham and Karen Walker have also been of great help.

When one does find that history, it tells a story of a city, a nation and a society under siege that ends with the destruction of all three. It has many different parts, including a magic city that seemingly sprang up overnight, a stolen locomotive, flaming buildings, columns of soldiers marching into the night, refugees fleeing into an unknown future and a new city still trying to come to grips with its past and its future simultaneously. This saga became the subject of a Pulitzer Prize–winning novel that inspired the most successful motion picture of all time, and it became the subject of the world's largest painting.

I remember as a child hearing a narrator explain that the men in the cyclorama who stood behind the cotton bales were Atlantans defending their city. That claim likely comes from a misunderstanding—those men were actually with the militia in the trenches during the Battle of Atlanta—but that sentiment still haunts me. The Gate City may have been a military objective, but for many people in 1864, it was also a home worth defending.

I wanted to add as a final chapter how a person could touch part of Atlanta's heritage. One can visit museums and exhibits on the Civil War, relive the Great Locomotive Chase, view *Gone With the Wind*, etc. Beyond that, the Atlanta of 1864, to paraphrase its great novel, survives only in the writings of the past. It has disappeared, except for what one today finds in reconstruction, replication, re-creation and display cases.

Had the Civil War centennial come ten years earlier, as documented in Franklin Garrett's monumental *Atlanta and Environs* (1952), when many of the area's important buildings of the Civil War were still standing, increased public interest might have saved them and contradicted something of the legend of the city's total destruction. Since 1954, however, still another Atlanta has been born, not from the ashes of war but in the dust of rapid growth, urban renewal and, as with the city's streets, progress without intelligible design.

I

THE GATE CITY

The great city that is Atlanta came into existence in the early 1840s, an era that would see the creation of numerous metropolises in the nation's true Midwest, from Pittsburgh to Dallas, built on the economic power of the steam technology of the new age. With the initial union of four railroads, what subsequently became the "Gate City" developed into the fastest-growing inland city in the Deep South. The city's first seal consisted of the image of a steam locomotive. Even during the Civil War, visitors would make the same complaint heard today that to get anywhere seemingly requires passing through Atlanta. Its State Square contained no courthouse, jail or monument but only Edward A. Vincent's magnificent railroad depot (built in 1856) and some of the city's enumerable trees. Critics complained that when the city hall/courthouse building went up on donated land, today occupied by the Georgia state capitol building, even it stood too far from the State Square, the true heart of the city. Despite the national debate over allowing slavery in the western lands taken in the war with Mexico, most of the South still awaited development for slavery and cotton. Railroads opened these new lands within, including along the new lines that intersected at Atlanta's State Square. For much of Georgia, this new city became the passage for goods coming in and cotton going out.

Geography, as a subject, concerns people doing the same things in the same place for the same reasons, often for millennia. Metropolitan archaeological remains along the south side of the Chattahoochee River show that ancient

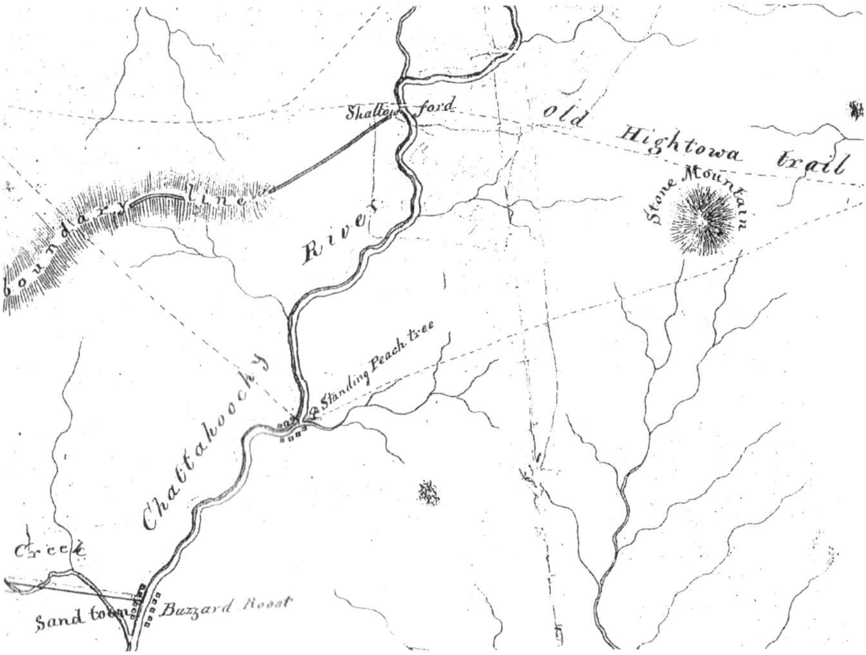

John Coffee drew this map showing the village of Standing Peachtree in 1829. *Courtesy National Archives and Records Administration, College Park, Maryland.*

peoples traveled in every direction for almost as long, relatively speaking, as human beings have been in the New World. These peoples included Mound Builders, wall builders and carvers of strange petroglyphs whose history we cannot know.

What became Atlanta first appears in our documentary records in 1782 as a mixed Cherokee and Creek Indian border community called Standing Peachtree along both sides of the Chattahoochee River where modern Peachtree Creek flows into the river. That site, according to historian Franklin M. Garrett, would in time become the namesake for the city's famed Peachtree Street and its other enumerable "Peachtree" names that would follow: "the Standing Peachtree has in truth covered the land with its descendents and provided the metropolis of the Southeast and its environs with a trade mark known the world over." Within this community there grew a peach tree atop an Indian burial mound, on the site where the city's modern waterworks now stand. In 1814, Lieutenant George Rockingham Gilmer of the Forty-third U.S. Infantry Regiment established Fort Standing Peachtree at that site to claim that important intersection for the United

George I. Parrish Jr.'s romanticized depiction of Lieutenant George R. Gilmer at the standing peach tree. *Courtesy the author.*

States during the dark days of the War of 1812. He wrote in his memoirs that he knew nothing about building a fort and, in fact, had never actually seen one.

The Creek Indians gave up the land that would become Atlanta and Fulton County with the Treaty of Indian Springs on January 8, 1821. On February 5, 1825, Standing Peachtree became the first post office subsequently established in Dekalb County. The postmasters were James McConnell Montgomery, one of the soldiers who had helped to build the earlier fort at the site and the operator of a ferry for crossing the river, and his sons. Around 1833, Hardy Ivy became the first white settler to build a home in what became Atlanta on his own land. By the early 1830s, Thomas Kile's grocery, a cabin home, a store and a blacksmith shop stood at a country intersection that had been the intersection of the Peachtree and Sandtown trails made by the local Indians. Nearby, Charner Humphries established the Whitehall Tavern of local legend that became one of Atlanta's first great historical losses, and the first of too many more, when it burned down during the Civil War.

In 1836, the state of Georgia gave up its ambitions for a canal to connect the shallow Chattahoochee River with the more substantial Tennessee. The plan changed to build one of the first railroads. Chief engineer Stephen Harriman Long considered several routes before settling on the practical and less expensive Montgomery's Ferry on the Chattahoochee, thus settling the terminus for the line in what would become Atlanta. The legislature assented to the location for the southern end of its railroad and also settled the site as the junction for connections to the private railroads being officially sponsored by the state to connect to the Georgia road by act on December 23, 1837. Ironically, the previously mentioned George R. Gilmer, now governor, would sign the bill. Called the Western & Atlantic (W&A), although it neither traveled west nor to the Atlantic, this railroad would, and still does, connect the Deep South to the lines that cross Tennessee and to the enormous network of track stretching across the Midwest. Indians, Irishmen and others did the necessary but difficult embankment work.

The community that sprang up at the southern end of the Western & Atlantic logically took the name of "Terminus." In 1842, Wilson Lumpkin, superintendent of the Western & Atlantic Railroad, and his engineer, Charles Fenton Mercer Garrett, claiming to have found better ground, moved the terminus of the railroad 132 yards west from where Long had set it in lot 78 to a new location in lot 77. The change rendered the Monroe Railroad's $25,000 embankment a waste of the failing railroad's last resources. Samuel

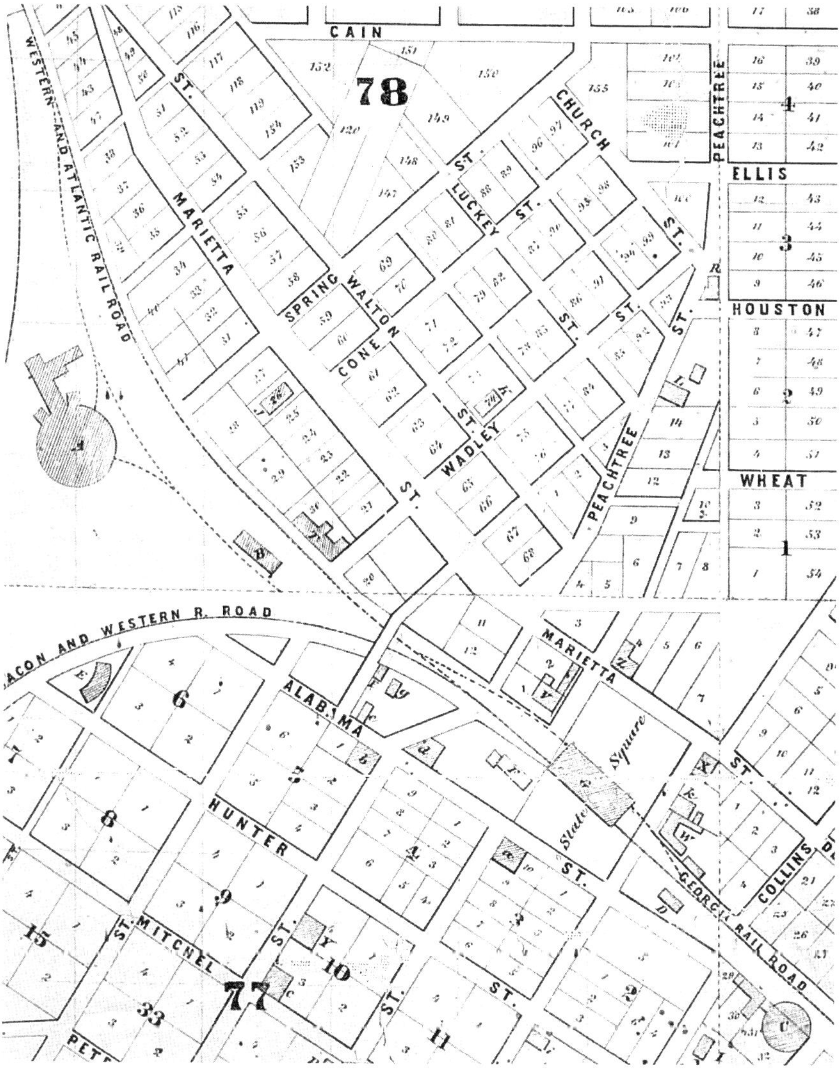

Five Points, the heart of old Atlanta, as depicted on Edward A. Vincent's 1853 map. *Courtesy Library of Congress.*

Mitchell, for whom Mitchell Street later took its name, donated five acres of land in lot 77 for the terminus of the W&A and what became State Square (today's Underground Atlanta). The change in the terminus also forced state workers to dig a gap through a ridge to connect the city's first railroads at the square. Despite Lumpkin's claims to the contrary, the ground for the new terminus was a swamp that required landfill. In 1852, the city council also had to create a bridge across the railroad yard (first named Bridge and later Broad Street) to allow citizens to pass safely from one side of the city to the other. In 1849, after Samuel Mitchell's death, a shadowy character representing the estate of the alleged real owner of lot 77 successfully sued to claim this land. Mitchell's heirs were able to pay him off, however.

That ground would subsequently become the heart of downtown Atlanta, with a junction of three roads that would become the city's legendary "Five Points." Marietta Street, Edgewood Avenue, Decatur Street, Peachtree Street and Whitehall Street (now the southern end of Peachtree Street) replaced this former intersection of two major Indian paths. Wilson Lumpkin, F.C. Arms and C.F.M. Garnett, in locating this tract for Mitchell, tried to reconcile this gift with the junction of the five roads, three ridges and the railroad. They thus inadvertently started the curious way in which, even today, the directions of the streets of Atlanta seem to defy any logic. The problem was exacerbated as original land lot owners would move the roads and streets in any way that suited them, creating what historian James Michael Russell describes as a legacy "of a tangle of messy intersections formed by streets meeting at odd angles." To add to this confusion, Mitchell's donation became the five-acre State Square (today's Underground Atlanta), where the railroads originally came together. It forced the city's leaders to arrange streets to accommodate this large open space in the middle of the city. In later years, as Franklin Garrett wrote, Atlanta's leaders added still more to the confusion as, for uncertain reasons, they renamed old streets that rightly honored the city's pioneers to names that had no discernable meanings.

Mitchell and Garnett named this intersection—which at that moment in 1842 had standing on it only a one-room shed that served as a train depot and a liquor store—"Marthasville," in honor of the daughter of Wilson Lumpkin. Aside from financially benefiting Mitchell by moving the railroad terminus, Wilson Lumpkin had helped survey the route for the now defunct canal project, worked tirelessly for the removal of the Cherokees from that route as governor and later supervised the building of the W&A. In 1845, this town had some one hundred people. Its incorporated and pretentious, but still recordless, government renamed it "Atlanta," most likely as shorthand for the Western & Atlantic as used by the Georgia Railroad's J. Edgar Thomson. Legend, however, has it named from Martha Lumpkin's middle name, "Atalanta" (from the Greek story of a female athlete and demigod daughter of Hades involved in a race with three golden apples).-

Many of the important men who were at this place from the beginning, such as chief engineers Stephen H. Long (Western & Atlantic) and J. Edgar

Thomson (Georgia Railroad), saw very little potential for this site, but they were quickly proven wrong. In 1847, Dr. William N. White, a visitor from Utica, New York, recorded in his journal that in just that summer, Atlanta had added 187 new buildings; in just eight months, it had added 30 large stores and 2 hotels. The latter could accommodate 150 persons each. By 1850, Atlanta had a population of 2,572, including 521 slaves. Aside from other businesses, the city had 57 stores.

That same year, the Western & Atlantic finally connected Atlanta to Chattanooga (the first locomotive, the Florida, had arrived the year before). The Gate City would, before the Civil War, also form a junction with the Georgia (1845, the longest railroad in the world when it was finished), the Monroe (1841, later reorganized as the Macon & Western) and the Atlanta & LaGrange (1851, renamed Atlanta & West Point) to become the hub for one-third of Georgia's twelve hundred miles of tracks. The most important tracks to connect with the city, the Memphis & Charleston, connected to the Western & Atlantic via the Nashville & Chattanooga at Chattanooga, Tennessee. In 1857, that connection, all of the same "southern" gage, added a connection between the Gate City and the Mississippi Valley. Not only did Atlanta thus become a railroad crossroads to the West, South and Midwest, but it also had the potential for one day being a critical junction on a transcontinental railroad.

Atlantans also dreamed and invested in even more tracks—a plan for an "Air Line" railroad, begun as a wood plank turnpike to Dahlonega (an idea similar to modern-day toll Highway 400), that would pass through northeast Georgia to new markets in Virginia and beyond. Engineer Lemuel P. Grant and businessman Jonathan Norcross envisioned it as a line that ultimately would stretch from New York to New Orleans. Economic downturns and the Civil War delayed its construction, as did competition for capital with Grant's project to build a Georgia Western Railroad to connect to the agricultural and mining resources of north Alabama. Atlantans also held meetings to plan another line that would have connected their city, by way of its link to Macon, to the Gulf Coast. The whole of this network would have made Atlanta the critical junction of a vast network of tracks that stretched from both of the coasts of northern Florida to all of the northern and midwestern United States.

Atlanta belonged to the great and growing steam cities of the true Midwest, but it also had unbreakable ties to the slave-produced cotton economy that made up 80 percent of the United States' exports before the Civil War. The Gate City's railroads and the surrounding cotton fields provide an example of what historian Edgar T. Thompson meant when he wrote of how a plantation economy resembles a mining town with all of the same problems of supply, labor and transportation.

Atlanta, by that standard, became a boomtown. So many bales of cotton came from it, and at such a rate, that by 1859, the Georgia Railroad alone annually sent some three thousand cars to the city empty. Profitable textile factories also went into operation at nearby Roswell and New Manchester. Increasingly, the merchants traded directly with New York City, thus avoiding the expense and the control of the merchant/planter intermediaries of the South's few ports. The Gate City also gave small farmers and ranchers direct access to northern capital that bypassed the politically and economically powerful planters.

The disparity in cargo did not make the transportation of goods to the city for local sale cheap. Individual railroads kept freight rates artificially high to Atlanta in order to support the cities, such as Savannah, that had helped to finance the railroads and, as with the state-owned Western & Atlantic Railroad, to make as high a profit as possible. Charleston and Savannah, the great Atlantic cotton ports, benefited even more from Atlanta's prosperity than did Atlanta. Atlanta's boosters protested the rates, but to no avail.

A city ordinance, however, taxed foodstuffs brought in by the railroads and thus encouraged local truck farming that made the city market a success and even expanded its dry goods and entertainment economies. (The twentieth century would see new growth in truck farming to the city that would eventually lead to the creation of the world's largest farmer's market.) Atlanta, although built on railroads, conversely succeeded in part by developing ways of successfully battling the restrictions imposed on it by those same railroads.

So much business went on in the Gate City that the situation became absurd. For example, H.G. Kuhrt's building boasted, among other businesses, a post office, a printing shop, two barbers, a bookbinder, a clothier, a bank, a lottery office and a restaurant, all sharing space. Similarly, according to Atlanta researcher Ken Denney, David Dougherty built what a sign on the outside identified as a "concert hall" but which seemingly housed everything but musical performances. Within its walls, Dougherty operated a restaurant and the city's first ten-pen hall. According to Denney's research, the building also served (at various times) as Dr. Needom L. Angier's office; Bell & Gaskill land office; William J. Cloud's piano store; the Macon & Western Telegraph Office; the Smith & Ezzard drugstore (open all night, if you rang the bell to wake up the night employee); the offices of the *Southern Confederacy* newspaper;

J.A. Thrasher, attorney; and W.W. Woodruff & Co., carriage repository. (During the Civil War, the building became a Confederate operations center that housed James J. Andrews and the other Federal saboteurs known as Andrews' Raiders who went to the gallows.) A visitor in 1862 observed:

> *Business seems to be the key note of all, and the point of sight in the picture of daily life. Horses are driven furiously through the streets; men dash along the pavements as if fearful of losing a customer, and even the women are "swift of foot," like ATLANTA* [Atalanta], *and hurry on as if the terrible gadfly of Jo were after them.*

A scheme by George Smith of Chicago to seize control of the economy of the Midwest by flooding the region with notes of the Atlanta Bank resulted in the bank losing its charter despite having solid assets. Atlantans responded by making their next bank locally owned.

Atlanta's so-called concert hall on the left. *Courtesy Library of Congress.*

By 1860, however, Atlanta had grown to a city of 7,741 people of diverse nationalities, origins and races. It had become the fourth-largest city in Georgia and had every prospect for further growth, having more than doubled in population in only a decade. The city had five wards, four fire companies, six banks, thirteen churches (black and white), a chamber of commerce, fifteen fire insurance agencies, five Masonic lodges, one gaslight company, more than forty lawyers, at least five newspapers (and a dozen other publications), fifteen manufactories, public schools, a poorhouse, one female academy and one medical college. It also boasted more than two hundred stores, retail establishments and offices of all types. Its hotels, each within convenient access to the State Square, included the Atlanta Hotel run by the jovial Dr. Joseph Thompson; Washington Hall, built and operated by James Loyd; and the four-story Trout House of Jeremiah F. Trout, to acclaim or criticism depending on the visitor. Atlanta offered every possibility to become the great railroad crossroads of the Southeast as the fastest-growing city in Georgia. In 1847 and 1854, Atlantans unsuccessfully campaigned for the removal to their city of the state capitol, then at Milledgeville. They enjoyed greater success by obtaining the annual state agricultural fair from Stone Mountain in 1850. Lemuel P. Grant donated ten acres on today's Memorial Drive, what was then named Fair Street, for the event. For a few years, the fair alternated annually between Atlanta and Macon until permanently finding a home in the Gate City in 1857.

Visitors would describe the city as so new that peanut shells, apple cores and mud lined its streets and sidewalks. All the great traveling entertainers, however, performed at Parr's Hall, a three-story walk-up, and later at the Atlanta Athenaeum, a structure used by its owners as a combination theater on the second floor and a grocery and feed warehouse on the first floor. Historian Russell Bonds wrote of it having everything seemingly from snake charmers to Shakespeare. Captain W.H. Barnes's famed concert company performed there, as did the Atlanta Amateurs, a local troupe of performers of music and drama. Tom Bethune (also Wiggins), a blind autistic slave who could mimic any music, became a sensation in Atlanta before he toured America and Europe.

Atlanta had other entertainments. Frenchman Antonio Maquino, near the resort of Anderson W. Walton (born in Augusta, Georgia, and a member of Atlanta's first city council) at the Walton Spring (now at the corner of Walton and Spring Streets), sold drinks and snacks. He also operated a primitive Ferris wheel type of contraption powered by two slaves. A shop at the mineral spring on Pryor Street, by the depot of the Macon & Western Railroad, also offered ice cream, sweetmeats, drinks and other knickknacks. Other entrepreneurs sold whiskey to make ends meet. Ormond's Grove at the end of Washington Street and Williams'/Durands' Mill on the south side of Peachtree Creek became popular for picnics. In the puritanical Gate City, however, dancing remained socially unacceptable, except among the students of the Atlanta Female Institute. They practiced waltzes, polkas, etc., as calisthenic exercises. No doubt, this training later helped them to win an impromptu marching competition against the best of a Confederate cavalry company. Far more thrilling for the citizens were the sometimes-weekly fires in the city and how any ride on the state-owned Western & Atlantic Railroad's 138 miles of track presented the all-too-real possibility of witnessing a train accident firsthand!

Atlantans seemingly represented every established state and European nation, as well as all recognized religions of mid-century 1800s America. The new metropolis on the shallow, rocky Chattahoochee River, however, had little crime or even disorderly conduct, legends and rumors to the contrary. The citizens had feared a slave revolt; Mayor John Norcross put down a rebellion by the Rowdy Party, which had seized an ancient cannon for use as an intended weapon of mass destruction; and the city's diverse people and newspaper editors argued issues of the day of the Native American Know-Nothing Party, the Democrats and the Whigs.

Atlanta's fire companies in 1856. *Courtesy Atlanta History Center.*

African Americans, free and slave, contributed most of the city's manual labor, although visitors found that the city had little of the slavery/plantation mentality or traditional planter aristocracy so often associated with the South. The city council, however, added additional restrictions, through local ordinances, to Georgia's already highly oppressive laws on the movements and activities of all of its black population. Any freedperson, for example, who moved to Atlanta had to pay a $200 fee for that privilege and $30 in annual fees, through white guardians, on pain of essentially having his or her labor sold by the city. Aside from concern about slave revolts, white Atlantans also feared the competition for jobs. The citizenry would not tolerate even the presence of freedman dentist Roderick Badger.

Because of state law and such ordinances, the city had only fifteen freedpersons in 1850 and twenty-five in 1860. Some African Americans avoided the laws against freedom, and others did not. Robert Webster was one of the city's successful businessmen, but he avoided the heavy fees and fines on freedpersons by remaining technically a slave. He would be among the citizen delegation that surrendered Atlanta to Sherman in 1864. During the Civil War, the city council rescinded the heavy tax that it had placed on African American mechanics, an ordinance originally aimed at the sixty-five skilled workers whom Ephraim G. Ponder (formerly of Thomasville, Georgia) hired out from his nearby plantation and factory. Although technically slaves, they were all but completely independent contractors. One of these workmen, Festus Flipper, was the father of Lieutenant Henry Ossian Flipper, later the first African American graduate of the United States Military Academy, and Reverend Joseph S. Flipper, future bishop of the African Methodist Episcopal Church. During the 1864 siege, Federal artillery fired on the Ponder Mansion and gardens, the finest, or almost the finest, grounds in the Atlanta area. The house reportedly took a ton of shot and shell. It never caught fire, but the damage proved so extensive that the Ponders never rebuilt it. On the other hand, Henry Long became a resident of the city after having achieved national notoriety upon his arrest in New York as one of the first escaped slaves apprehended under the Fugitive Slave Act of 1850. In 1854 in Atlanta, he waited on Millard Fillmore, the former president who had signed the act that cost him his freedom.

Everyone seemed to be some sort of entrepreneur in building this city, although with varying degrees of success. Some of the city's leaders, like Lemuel Pratt Grant (of Maine, gave the land for today's Grant Park), John Edgar Thomson (of Pennsylvania, later famed president of the Pennsylvania Railroad who came up with the name "Atlanta") and Richard Peters (of

Edward A. Vincent's 1853 map. *Courtesy Library of Congress.*

Pennsylvania), had stayed on after building the railroads. William Markham (of Connecticut) arrived in 1853. He soon became mayor and, with his brother-in-law, Thomas W. Healey (of Connecticut), would boast that he literally built Atlanta, or at least some one hundred of its businesses and other structures. He and his partners, Lewis Blake (of Indiana) and James Schofield (of Connecticut), bought the Atlanta Rolling Mill from Dr. L.A. Douglas of Indiana and Frazier & Company of Richmond, Virginia. It served as one of the South's few foundries for rolling railroad tracks and sheet metal, although the railroads declined to buy its products, claiming that the Georgia iron ore used as filler made the tracks too brittle. Its more than one hundred workers produced $137,230 worth of iron goods in 1860 alone. The city also had two railroad machine shops, as well as two iron foundries/machine shops—one established by Joseph Winship (of Massachusetts) and the other by inventor Austin Leyden (of Pennsylvania) and early Georgia industrialist Robert Findlay (of Scotland and Pennsylvania). Richard Peters built a steam-powered flour mill, the largest south of Richmond. It ultimately failed, however, due to the high freight rates charged by the railroads for wheat. The metropolitan area also had tanneries, shoe shops, various clothing establishments and sawmills that would make the city a supply depot for the manufacturing-starved Confederate States of America. Trees, creeks and hills, however, crowded Atlanta in such a way that the Union soldiers, in 1864, would find it hard to believe that a city existed somewhere in this great forest, some parts of which remain uncut even to the present day.

Some Atlantans, however, did not fare well in the city's rise. Insurance agent Green Jones Foreacre (of Ohio), for example, had a reputation as a swindler. Native Georgian George Washington Lee of nearby Stone Mountain represented the city's would-be wealthy. He had little to show for years of trying his hand as a millwright, real estate speculator, grocer and bartender with various partners, except the goodwill of many other men who had also gambled on the future of the "Gate City." According to historian James Michael Russell, only a small part of the city's population benefited from this chase after wealth. In 1850, for example, he found that only 0.5 percent of the adult citizenry owned 43 percent of the real estate, and 80 percent owned no property at all. By 1858, only 1.6 percent of the population held 55 percent of the real estate.

These destitute, wealthy, criminal, respected, slave and free lived, died and were buried in proximity to one another, a situation of societal intimacy that would last, at least along racial lines, until almost the mid-twentieth century. As historian Franklin Garrett pointed out, the city's Oakland Cemetery stood next to, and not away from, the railroad tracks and the site of the supporting stores, warehouses, foundries and factories from which the living staked their fortunes. Georgia's legislature created Fulton County, with Atlanta as the county seat, on December 20, 1853. Dr. Needom L. Angier, native of New Hampshire and future mayor of Atlanta, named the new county for transportation pioneer Robert Fulton, although sometimes the honor goes to Hamilton Fulton, the engineer who, with Wilson Lumpkin, had roughly surveyed for the canal that preceded the survey for the Western & Atlantic Railroad.

Some people only briefly passed through the new city on a hill in its early days, to leave milestones and then quickly pass on. Later Georgia political giant Alexander H. Stephens, for example, first stopped there briefly in

1839, just long enough to envision the great metropolis to come. Tennessee tinsmith Moses W. Formwalt became Atlanta's first mayor with the pro-alcohol voting block in 1848 but died from a knife attack while serving as a deputy sheriff and escorting a prisoner from the city council chambers in 1852. The young Englishman Edward Arista Vincent, creator of the city's first official map and designer of the city's elegant depot and railroad car shed, would join him in Oakland Cemetery four years later. General Sherman would use the 1853 Vincent map to lay siege to the city in 1864 and would subsequently destroy the depot out of military necessity.

The 1853 railroad terminal at the State Square, designed by Edward Vincent, as it appeared in 1864. It was one hundred feet wide and three hundred feet long. *Courtesy Library of Congress.*

Today, by appointment, a visitor can visit the replica of Fort Standing Peachtree on the grounds of the city's waterworks and, with similar difficulty near today's Underground Atlanta (the site of the original State Square), visit the Zero Mile Post that marked the beginning of the Western & Atlantic Railroad and what became Atlanta. An 1840s farm and a common plantation house of the period stand at the Atlanta History Center, but the most common memorial to the first years of what became the great city remains in its street names. Peachtree Battle, Howell's Mill, William's Mill, West Pace's Ferry, etc., speak for themselves, but as historian Franklin Garrett wrote, the real monument to the pioneers remains the names of such streets as Calhoun, Collins, Forsyth, Ivy, Luckie, Peters and Pryor, among others.

II

First Flag of the Confederacy

The diversity of the small but rapidly growing city allowed for a variety of opinions about the coming crisis that became the American Civil War. Throughout the South, however, the persons who most controlled and profited from cotton, America's greatest single export in those years, controlled the press, pulpit and politicians of the slave states. Atlanta had lively public gatherings on the issues of the day, but as the slave states grew weaker politically on the national stage, any perceived challenge to slavery became intolerable to Southerners, who depended directly or indirectly on cotton for their livelihoods and future. In 1849, for example, the wildly popular Georgia politician Alexander H. Stephens from Crawfordville nearly died from knife wounds inflicted in Atlanta by a political opponent who demeaned Stephens's call for compromise with the North as treason to the South. Similarly, in 1850, a Macon editor reprinted, from an Atlanta newspaper, an anonymous letter by Atlantan Cornelius Redding Hanleiter that reported on local criticism of the opening of a new slave market. A mob subsequently threatened to burn down the offices of the Macon newspaper and warned its Kentucky-born and slave-owning editor to leave town forever.

Enthusiasts for a Southern nation had nothing of that kind of violence to fear. The majority of Atlanta's electorate voted for the moderate Unionist John Bell for president in 1860, but loud voices for independence would soon after drown out the moderates in the Gate City and across Georgia. On October 30, Dr. W.F. Westmoreland formed the "Minute Men of

Criticism of the opening of this slave market in Atlanta in 1856 nearly caused a riot and the destruction of a newspaper office in Macon. *Courtesy Library of Congress.*

Fulton County," a political and quasi-military company to defend Southern rights against an abolitionist national government and to support secession. Eventually this group would total more than two hundred men.

Upon news of Abraham Lincoln's election in early November 1860, a statewide debate raged, not as much between secessionists and Unionists as between the people who would leave the United States immediately and those who would wait to see the results of coming events. In Atlanta, the Minute Men, wearing Revolutionary War–style cockades, set out to win converts for leaving the Union immediately. Enthusiasts for this revolution had names of persons said to be "submissionists" stricken from the ballot in the city election. English-born Atlanta resident Samuel Richards recorded in his diary that the loudest voices for secession came from young professionals who had nothing to lose from the war and politicians playing on popular anger to gain votes. He confided those opinions to his diary, however.

On December 22, Atlanta had a day of celebration upon the news of South Carolina's decision to leave the Union. The Minute Men celebrated by marching through the streets while firing salutes from cannons and small arms. Politicians gave speeches calling for independence for Georgia with the boast that it would happen without any spilling of blood. Across the city, citizens drank salutes to secession. A torchlight parade ended with a crowd burning an effigy of Abraham Lincoln in front of the Planter's Hotel. Ten days later, Atlanta's secessionist delegates defeated their moderate opposition by two to one in an election to represent Fulton County in the upcoming convention at Milledgeville to decide the state's future. Almost as if a symbol of the times, the next day the city shook from a minor earthquake.

Across Georgia, the immediate secessionists failed to do as well, but they were still an overwhelming presence at the convention. Overall, the delegates from across the state voted for secession 209 to 89 on January 19, 1861, making Georgia the fifth state to secede from the Union. In the Gate City, the news brought more speeches, parades, bonfires and toasts. Opponents to this immediate secession, however, included Alexander H. Stephens of Crawfordville, a powerful and popular political speaker during his many trips to Atlanta, who would nonetheless later serve as the Confederacy's vice president; and attorney James M. Calhoun, the man who, as the city's mayor, would have to surrender Atlanta to Sherman in 1864.

Almost immediately, concerns grew about security for the newly independent Georgia, both internally and externally. A Fulton County grand jury called for a mustering of the local militia. The city's four fire companies, although exempt from military and jury duty, offered their services for local security and patrol duty. Atlantans had already formed volunteer military companies, starting with the Atlanta Irish Volunteers, whose officers, commissioned on January 24, 1854, were Captain Allison Nelson, First Lieutenant Beman T. Lamb, Second Lieutenant Thomas T. Daniel and Third Lieutenant Louis Valentine. The Gate City Guard received commissions in March 1859 but formally incorporated on December 14, 1859, under Captain George Harvey Thompson, First Lieutenant William L. Ezzard, Second Lieutenant S.W. Jones and Third Lieutenant John H. Lovejoy. Each member wore a formal uniform of dark blue trimmed in gold, with a black French shako complete with white plume, but a service uniform of gray. A third company, the Atlanta Grays, organized in July 1859, with Captain Alexander M. Wallace, First Lieutenant George H. Daniel, Second Lieutenant U.P. Carson, Third Lieutenant S.B. Love and Fourth Lieutenant B.M. Smith. With Georgia's secession, the city also acquired the service of the City Light Guards under Captain George G. Hull, First Lieutenant J. Thompson, Second Lieutenant Warren Jourdan, Third Lieutenant William F. Pick and Fourth Lieutenant Harry Krouse; the Fulton Dragoons under Captain William T. Wilson (later B.C. Yancey), First Lieutenant Zachariah A. Rice and Second Lieutenant William M. Williams; and the Jackson Guards under Captain James H. Neal, First Lieutenant Dennis S. Myers, Second Lieutenant John P. Kelly and Junior Second Lieutenant Peter Fenlon Jr.

George Washington Lee in his militia dress uniform before the Civil War. *From the Lee/Huss Family Papers, AC 69-249, courtesy Georgia Archives, Morrow.*

None of these units would have anything like the history of Atlanta's "Georgia Volunteers." Major George Washington Lee, commander of the Peachtree militia battalion and de facto commander of the Fulton County militia, formed this company from his fellow mechanics and lodge members of Masonic Lodge No. 59, men made unemployed by the prewar national economic recession. Other officers included First Lieutenant John R. Rhodes, Second Lieutenant John W. Brown and Junior Second Lieutenant William McConnell. With the help of the city's most prominent men, Lee sought to obtain acceptance of his unit by Governor Joseph E. Brown so that his men, whom he described as poor, might be paid. Overrun with more companies than he could supply from across the state and likely confusing Lee with a Florida con man also known as Major Lee, the governor did not respond. The Atlantan then took his men to Montgomery, Alabama, and successfully offered his volunteers as the first military unit of the army of the newly created Confederate government. Ladies traveling with the company acquired material in Grantville and made what became the first Confederate flag in Georgia. Lee's men would join the Gate City Guards in the unsuccessful siege of Fort Pickens near Pensacola, Florida. Lee's 109 men did valuable engineering work in handling the 113 cannons used in the siege. Braxton Bragg, the Confederate commander at Pensacola, would highly compliment Lee and his men, although two years later in Atlanta the general would forget those words and would claim that he had felt differently about Lee.

Atlanta and Fulton County took the lead in Georgia in supplying companies for the new Confederate army, with at least a dozen in the early months of the war, as well as at least 150 other men for the Southern army. Another dozen companies would follow, including state and local defense forces such as the city's German Steuben Yeagers, Silver Grays, Atlanta Volunteers, Ordnance Guards and Raid Repellers. By the end of the war, Fulton County gave at least 2,660 men to the Confederate army.

Citizens celebrated the marching to war of every local company and even greeted the many more who passed through the city. The seventy-five-member Gate City Guards, for example, left for Pensacola on April 1. Despite a steady rain, the largest crowd assembled in Atlanta's brief history

George W. Lee and his company of Atlanta mechanics at Pensacola. The mortar in the middle fired the first shot against Fort Sumter. *From the* Photographic History of the Civil War, *courtesy Bob Bradley*.

A Southern soldier leaves for war. *Courtesy Library of Congress.*

cheered them on. The young ladies of the Atlanta Female Academy led the honors by presenting each soldier with a paper Confederate flag, and Miss J.E. Hanleiter presented the unit with a cloth Confederate flag. The men returned the kindness with a gift of a ladies' gold watch. T.R.R. Cobb, soon after a Confederate general, gave the men a stirring speech.

Sallie Conley Clayton, one of the paper flag presenters, would remember the send-off given for Captain Green J. Foreacre's "Confederate Volunteers" company at a crowded Atlanta Athenaeum in early June 1861, following, as usual, music provided by Captain Barnes's concert group. After the presentation of a flag by Miss Caroline Yancey, Captain Foreacre addressed the crowd and then gave the flag to the color-bearer, Fourth Sergeant William G. Fishback, admonishing him to "never allow its folds to trail in the dust." The sergeant, loudly and with a pause between each word, shouted, "Never! Never! Never!" The crowd went wild and could only be calmed down by the orchestra.

Throughout 1861, as both nations prepared for a long war, Atlanta civilians did their part. A committee of safety formed groups to care for the families of soldiers, and the city's doctors offered free medical care to the destitute families of men who had left to fight. The faculty of the city's

One of the paper flags given out by Sallie Clayton and other women to departing soldiers. *Courtesy Nicholson Family Papers, Atlanta History Center.*

Medical College converted their building from a school to a military hospital. Governor Joseph E. Brown held a convention in the city to organize private gun manufacturers, and he offered the use of the forges of the state-owned Western & Atlantic Railroad to make gun barrels.

The city sought, however, to be far more for the new Southern nation. When the Confederate Provincial Congress first met in Montgomery, Alabama, Atlantans campaigned to move even this temporary government to their city and, with the creation of the new nation, lobbied to have their Gate City made the permanent capital of the Confederate States of America. Both efforts failed, as did the city's earlier attempt to become the state capital (it did achieve that goal in 1868, however). Despite Atlanta's central location, transportation and security, Richmond became the Confederate capital. Although located less than one hundred miles from Washington, D.C., the Virginia city held half of the Southern nation's manufacturing, its only two cannon factories, the junction of critical railroad transportation and the only foundries with a relatively local supply of coal and iron. The new nation could not and did not last long without Richmond. President Jefferson Davis and Vice President Alexander H. Stephens, however, did separately visit the Gate City shortly after their inauguration.

Contrary to widely published legend, Atlanta was not "second only to Richmond" as a Confederate manufacturing center or the Confederacy's "second city," although it did contribute at least its share to the manufacturing-strapped Confederacy, as did other cities and depots across the South. It did have the Atlanta Rolling Mill, the only foundry outside of Richmond for making or refurbishing railroad tracks. That foundry would roll the iron plates for all, or almost all, of the Confederacy's iron warships, including for the ill-fated *Atlanta*, a Scottish-built ship converted to an ironclad by the Southern navy and captured near Savannah on June 17, 1863. Such expensive vessels defended the South's few ports by their intimidating appearance more than by real combat power. Critics argued that the warships wasted resources better used slowing the decline of the South's railroads, in tracks, tires and other railroad iron. The city's manufacturing establishments did get a boon when the machinery from the works in Nashville moved to Atlanta to escape the capture of the former city by Federal troops in February 1862. The Gate City's prewar shoe manufacturing provided some of the badly needed footwear and harness for the Southern armies, thanks to cobblers and harness workers detailed from the ranks to work in Atlanta.

The city did become one of the major supply depots in the Confederate States of America, for both the South's army and navy. Office space for its many agencies became scarce as it all but took over the city's center. Historian Ken Denney has compiled a military directory based on varying newspaper accounts of the Atlanta offices of the Confederate government:

City Military Directory

(Based on the Daily Intelligencer *of May 1864 and* Southern Confederacy *newspaper of June 1864)*

Confederate

Major General Howell Cobb, Commanding District of Georgia and Florida; Office Whitehall Street, upstairs, four doors north of Hunter Street

Colonel M.H. Wright, Commanding Troops and Defenses, Atlanta Office over Atlanta Insurance and Banking Co., near Railroad

Post of Atlanta

Major General Marcus J. Wright, Commandant of Post; Office, Marietta Street, Brumby Building

Captain Charles W. Peden, Provost Marshal; Office, Whitehall Street above Alabama

Georgia Reserves

Brigadier General Lucius J. Gartrell, Commanding Reserves at Atlanta; Office, Lynch's Building, Whitehall Street

Major G.M. Proctor, Quartermaster, Georgia Reserves; Office near Hunter and Whitehall Streets

Captain F.M. Johnston, Assistant Quartermaster, Georgia Reserves; Office near corner of Hunter and Whitehall streets

Ordnance Department

Colonel M.H. Wright, Chief commanding Arsenal; Office over Atlanta Insurance and Banking Co.

Lieutenant John Ansly, Military storekeeper; Office, Wyly Building, Peachtree Street

Naval Department

Lieutenant McCorkle, Commanding Naval works and T. Alphonse Jackson, Chief Engineer, CSN; Office, Marietta Street, next to Dr. Bean, Dentist

Engineer's Department

Captain L.P. Grant, Chief Engineer; Office, Lynch's Building, corner Whitehall and Alabama streets

Lieutenant J.W. Glenn, Engineer officer; Office, Lynch's Building

Pay Department

Lieutenant Colonel A.J. Smith, Chief, Army of Tennessee; Office, Marietta Street, near First Presbyterian Church

Major A.B. Hagan, Pay Quartermaster for Post; Office on Whitehall Street, south of Mitchell

Captain B.F. Bomar, Assistant Paymaster Quartermaster Post; Office on Whitehall Street, south of Mitchell

Quartermaster's Department

Major G.W. Cunningham, Clothing; Office Alabama Street, one door east of Whitehall

Major W.M. Bacon, Chief, Tax in Kind; Office over Central Railroad Bank, Alabama Street

Major H.T. Massengale, Quartermaster Post; Office, Herring's Building, Whitehall Street

Major G.R. Fairbanks, Hospital Quartermaster; Office over McNaught & Ormond, Whitehall Street

Major J.P. Horbach, Office east side Whitehall Street

Major Throckmorton, Quartermaster

Captain J.A. Anderson, Inspector Field Transportation; Office next to E.M. Edwardy's, Whitehall Street

Transportation Department

Captain John Frizzell, Chief; Office corner of Whitehall and Alabama Streets

Captain J.T. Peyton (local, per Daily Intelligencer*); Office, corner of Whitehall and Mitchell streets (Office, Roark Street, corner Whitehall—per* Daily Intelligencer*)*

Commissary Department

Major J.F. Cummings, Chief; Office Whitehall Street, near Alabama, up stairs

Major F.R. Shackelford, Post Commissary; Office over McNaught and Ormond, Whitehall Street

Major R.T. Wilson, Chief, Department East Tennessee; (Office with Major Cummings—per Daily Intelligencer*)*

Captain W.R. Cox, Depot Commissary; Office, Whitehall Street near post office (opposite to Post Office, per Daily Intelligencer*)*

Nitre and Mining Bureau

Captain F.H. Smith, Office on Western and Atlantic Railroad, one mile from depot.

Medical Department

Surgeon E.H. Stout, Medical Director of Hospitals; Office, Whitehall Street, below Mitchell

Surgeon J.P. Logan; Senior Surgeon, Post; Office over Hunnicutt and Taylor's Drug Store, Peachtree Street

Surgeon G.S. Blackie, Medical Purveyor; Office, Peachtree Street over Clarke's Hardware Store

Assistant Surgeon J.F. Young, Medical Purveyor; Office Peachtree Street, opposite Ordnance Office

Conscript Department

(Additional position, per Daily Intelligencer*: Major G.W. Lee, Assistant Adjutant General; Office, Confederacy Building)*

Lieutenant G.A. Cabanniss (In May, the position was occupied by Lieutenant J.M. Harwell, per Daily Intelligencer*), Enrolling officer 8th District; Office, Masonic Hall, Decatur Street*

(In May, the position had been occupied by Major G.W. Lee) Lieutenant W.A. Thomas, Sub-Enrolling Officer, Fulton County; in Rawson's Building, Whitehall Street

State

Gov. Joseph E. Brown, Commander in Chief; Rawson's Building, corner Whitehall and Hunter Streets

(Additional position, per Daily Intelligencer*, listed under Conscript Department:) Colonel Sam Holt, Aid de Camp to the Governor; Office Whitehall Street, next door to the Provost Marshal's office.)*

Major General H.C. Wayne, Adjutant and Inspector General; Second floor, Markham Building, Whitehall Street

Major G.W. Speers, Quartermaster Division; Office, same

Colonel Cleghorn, Ordnance Officer; Whitehall Street, second door above Alabama
Major General G.W. Smith, Commanding Georgia Militia
State Quartermaster's Department
Colonel Ira R. Foster, Quartermaster General; Office near Corner Whitehall and Alabama streets, upstairs
Captain V.A. Gaskill, Leather and Shoes; Office near Corner Whitehall and Hunter Streets, first floor
Captain J.A.R. Hanks; Clothing; Office near Corner Whitehall and Hunter streets, first floor
C.M. Wellborn, Military Storekeeper; Office on Peachtree Street
State Commissary Department
Colonel Jared I. Whitaker, Commissary General, Office: corner Whitehall and Alabama streets
Captain William Watkins, Purchasing Commissary, Office: Brown's old stand on Whitehall Street
A.B. Forsyth, Military storekeeper, Office on Alabama Street
Jesse M. Butt, State Salt Agent, Office, corner Whitehall and Marietta streets

Private and government manufactories made pikes, railroad cars, dental supplies, Bibles and much more. E.N. Spiller and J.H. Burr made Colt model pistols. W.S. Withers and Solomon Solomon made spurs, buckles, etc., while the Atlanta Machine Works made ordnance. One steam-powered plant turned the bones from the local burial site for dead horses and mules into buttons. The Confederacy opened a remount depot on Trinity Avenue in downtown and eventually, reportedly, impressed every available horse and mule of any value for the Army of Tennessee. Atlanta's Quartermaster Department, under George W. Cunningham, made all manner of clothes for the army and eventually employed twenty-seven male cutters and three thousand seamstresses to make some ninety thousand uniforms per month by April 1863. His shoemaking operation employed three dozen workers and could make, based on available leather, up to five hundred pairs of shoes a day. The city's banks grew in number, and each came to hold large sums of the treasury notes of both the State of Georgia and the Confederate States of America. The banks closed during the siege of 1864 and never reopened. Lemuel P. Grant even revived his idea of a western railroad to connect Atlanta to the iron and coal resources of Alabama. His Rome &

Blue Mountain Railroad, however, ultimately failed from no access to the South's declining supply of tracks.

Colonel Marcus H. Wright's Atlanta Arsenal became the city's most extensive operation during the Civil War. Throughout the city, thirteen shops of this operation made ammunition for small arms and artillery.

A leather shop made its harness and saddles. Contractors made other goods for the arsenal. It became the city's largest employer, with 5,464 men and women. Finding skilled workers and keeping employees in these manufactories became a crisis, with the Confederacy's low wages and the rising prices in Atlanta. The Arsenal also faced constant problems with shortages of materials but still produced, just between July 1, 1862, and June 30, 1863, 23,000,000 pistol and musket caps; 4,100,000 rounds of small arms ammunition; 286,000 friction primers; 719 sets of artillery harness; 2,124 cavalry saddles; 2,031 bridles; 11,801 cartridge boxes; 17,796 cap boxes; 13,334 cartridge box belts; 8,188 waist boxes; 9,312 tin canteens; and 87,177 priming tubes.-

Not every effort became a positive contribution, however. Green J. Foreacre tried unsuccessfully to sell the government wooden bowls. The Rushton Company made four revolutionary breech-loading cannons that reportedly had a successful trial at Stone Mountain and four batteries of rifled artillery fired from tripods for Wright's Legion. Colonel Augustus R. Wright wanted these weapons demonstrated before government officials in Richmond. When the heavy guns later proved defective in Savannah, the Rushton Company went out of the artillery business, and apparently its only additional contribution to the government was one set of scales.

Except for the confusion in the streets caused by the constant passing of officials, soldiers, trains and wagons, the city knew relative peace its first year. Atlanta's Gate City Guards and Atlanta Grays would suffer dead and wounded in the battles of the summer of 1861, but for Atlantans the war became something infinitely more than heroic speeches, fanfare and soldiers' traditional complaints one year later. Casualty lists by then filled whole pages of Atlanta's newspapers for the first time. Colonel George W. Lee had rushed the Thirty-eighth Georgia Volunteer Infantry, 1,050 men strong, and many of his fellow Atlantans to Virginia that June, but by the following September the regiment had only 35 men still standing. On October 16, 1862, D.C. Smith, the local enrolling officer, ordered all able-bodied men between the ages of eighteen and thirty-five to report

Previous page: Some of George N. Barnard's photographs of Civil War Atlanta after its occupation by Federal troops in September 1864. *Courtesy Library of Congress.*

to him. He assured the public that he had such force as needed to arrest any man in Fulton County who failed to comply.

By the spring of 1863, the deteriorating military situation brought the war to the doorsteps of Atlantans. The campaign in Mississippi created a flood of deserters who headed east through Georgia en route to their homes. In June 1861, Atlanta's city hall had already become a makeshift jail for seven hundred wildly dressed and rowdy Zouave soldiers from Pensacola. When they began to escape, officials had them transported to Decatur. They received a breakfast there and proved to be gentlemen. In the first week of July 1863, the Confederate armies lost fifty thousand men in defeats at Port Hudson, Louisiana; Vicksburg, Mississippi; and Gettysburg, Pennsylvania. Late in the summer, Confederate soldiers from the surrender of Vicksburg showed up in Atlanta nearly naked, barefoot and without money. Being on parole, they found themselves dismissed from the army until they received exchange for Federal soldiers held in Richmond. Many civilians feared that without help these men would take what they needed out of desperation. Already disillusioned by the war, many of the Vicksburg parolees felt abandoned by their government and announced that, if exchanged, they would desert rather than return to their units. Among the efforts made on their behalf, the Atlanta Ladies' Hospital Association gave one thousand of these veterans a dinner.

In May 1863, when Federal colonel Abel Streight's raid in Alabama threatened Georgia, then captain George W. Lee moved to protect Rome with the few remaining men in his Atlanta security force and two pieces of artillery. He subsequently wrote to his superiors that although Atlanta served as one of the Confederacy's important supply depots, in the case of another panic, he might face as many as five thousand enemy soldiers. So many of his men had been taken by the army, after having been promised exemption from the draft, that he doubted he could now find more than one hundred men for a defense force. Even five hundred Yankee raiders could take the city, he warned, and render this Southern terminal of the vital Western & Atlantic Railroad useless.

That panic had hardly passed when a Federal army under General William S. Rosecrans marched on Atlanta. Almost every white male civilian of any military value found himself forced into some form of six-month duty unit, including the fire department and the railroad workers. The Union army fled back to Chattanooga following defeat by the Confederate troops of General Braxton Bragg and General James Longstreet at the Battle of Chickamauga on September 19–20, 1863.

This Pyrrhic victory, fought only some 120 miles from Atlanta, created more than 14,600 wounded. The city's military hospitals, including the building erected at the fairgrounds, had only eighteen hundred beds. By the end of the war, Atlantans hosted estimated totals of 80,000 Confederate and 25,000 Union wounded brought to the city. Eventually, it would be second only to Richmond as a hospital center. Sick soldiers would break quarantine and spread disease among the civilians. Medical stores had to have guards. Moonshiners smuggled whiskey into the city on the pretense of supplying the hospitals.

By 1864, the citizenry walked blocks to avoid the great open park by the train depot that the hotels faced in State Square, today's Underground Atlanta. It had become flooded with wounded left in the open air, as re-created in the 1939 motion picture *Gone With the Wind*. The churches and hotels around the square, as well as the Medical College, the Female Institute and several other buildings, became hospitals, adding to the city's shortage of shelter. Tents housed the overflow of wounded and sick.

Some planters sent their wives and daughters to work in the hospitals to avoid their slaves becoming sick doing that duty. (Sales and prices for slaves grew and became the best, or one of the best, investments in the city.) During the smallpox epidemic, Atlanta officials set up a special quarantine hospital for the slaves.

Donations of goods and money for the military hospitals came from individuals and charitable groups, black and white, in the Atlanta area. The Atlanta Amateurs toured and also performed at the Atlanta Athenaeum, as did other groups, to raise funds for the hospitals. Ladies of the Atlanta Hospital Association met every train load of wounded to reach the city and shared whatever could be spared for the suffering men, many of whom would soon come to lie in the city's Oakland Cemetery. Martha Winship, after the arrival of the first waves of wounded following the Battle of Shiloh in 1862, converted her home into a hospital with her black coachman, Booker, as her "surgeon in chief." Patients lucky enough to be assigned to her home received exceptional care. A tribute to her memory and her service as president of the Atlanta Hospital Association told of the work of the women in the city's many hospital relief organizations:

> *Long trains of cattle cars loaded with dead and dying, with naked and starving, with sick and wounded were arriving at all hours. Not a train arrived but was met by these women...who hastened with first aid, with hot coffee and food.*

These same Atlantans also donated to the city's soldiers in the field. Ladies knitted socks, made pants, prepared homemade foods and raised money. Citizen groups even sent the city's soldiers spittoons, catsup, towels and bottles of wine. Unlike in Macon, however, the local churches declined the public request for their bronze bells for use in making cannons.

Many Atlantans found reasons to believe in the Confederate cause to the end. When famed cavalryman General John H. Morgan came to Atlanta on February 6, 1864, after having escaped from a penitentiary in Ohio, he became a local celebrity. Atlantans gave him and his wife the largest parade held in the city to that date. At one point, men from the crowd of thousands took the place of horses in pulling his carriage. Morgan would make Atlanta his headquarters and recruiting station. It and nearby Decatur became a refuge for his fellow Kentuckians.

For Atlanta and life behind the lines in the Confederacy, Alexander H. Stephens's observations two years earlier would prove on mark:

> *Revolutions are much easier started than controlled, and the men who begin them, even for the best purposes and objects, seldom end them…The selfish, the ambitious, and the bad will generally take the lead.*

III

The City that Went to War against Itself

Historians argue that the American conflict between 1861 and 1865 did not constitute the modern definition of a civil war but rather was a war of independence by the Southern states. Atlanta, with its diverse population, certainly had patriotic secessionists making heroic sacrifices for the Southern cause. Within the city's growing numbers of people, however, there also arose a genuine civil war by anyone's definition as the fighting increasingly turned against the South and the Gate City steadily came under siege, first strategically and later literally. As one person who escaped to the Federal lines would remember:

> *If the war continues four years longer, it seems to me those* [in Atlanta] *who escape deaths from bullets or pestilence must die of excitement, for there you see nothing but war. You eat war; you hear war; you talk nothing but war; and when you retire to your bed you dream of war. You wake tired of war but the despot has you by the throat, with a thousand bayonets bristling round you, and you must fight or do worse.*

Patriotism in Civil War Atlanta, like everything else, became a commodity sold for the highest price. Food prices soared during the bitterly cold winter of 1863; flour cost $35 per barrel, shoes were $500 per pair and eggs were $1 per dozen. At the same time, the value of Confederate currency declined so rapidly that Atlantans bought books and other nonperishables to launder their inflating money. Lucy Harvie Hull remembered the currency becoming

Wilbur Kurtz's painting of what Atlanta might have looked like in 1860. *Courtesy Atlanta History Center.*

so worthless that she wished for $100 to buy candy, only to have her father angrily hand her the cash and challenge her to find a stick of candy in Confederate Atlanta for even that price.

Profiteering from this situation made more than twenty Atlantans the then enormous sum of over $100,000 by November 1862. A Northern sympathizer wrote in June 1864 that without the sacrifices of the women for the hospitalized soldiers, "the rebellion would have broken down ere this." He then added:

> *While many* [persons] *have thus been laboring, others, in Atlanta in particular, have been riding in their four thousand dollar carriages, dressed in thousand dollar silks and two thousand dollar cloaks, and at night attending the theatre or joining in the dance for John Morgan or some other hero.*

Life for other Atlantans became very different. Poor men, forced into the Confederate service by the draft, complained bitterly of the politically powerful buying substitutes or otherwise obtaining exemptions from military service. Even Atlanta's newspapers had the Atlanta Press Guards, a company of newspaper employees exempt from the draft. They offered membership to anyone willing to pay $500. By the autumn of 1862, only six months after the war had begun, Atlanta's newspapers already reported the desperate efforts of the army to obtain shoes locally and carried pleas for clothes for the local regiments serving in Virginia. In Atlanta, however, for the civilians, prices for such commodities soared.

Even circumstances waged war against the average citizen. A shortage of rolling stock reduced shipments of food to the city from Tennessee, but then a wartime drought in north Georgia and the unusually cold winter of 1863–64 killed regional crops and livestock. Hog cholera in Georgia in 1863 further cut into the livestock. Inflation and the usurping of wood by the Atlanta Arsenal made the cold weather far worse for the city's population. Atlantans brought their livestock into their homes during the winter to protect the animals from the cold but also from theft by hungry neighbors. Murder and robbery rates soared. Prices in stores rose so high that families with anything left to trade bartered for meats and produce from the "Crackers," the poor, yellow-skinned, rural Georgians in the covered wagons that passed through the streets of Atlanta. Even that access to food declined when impressments by the Confederate army frightened the independent farmers out of the city. Local businesses tried to expand upon and simplify the growing barter system by issuing their own currency, or "shinplasters."

Across the Confederacy, in the spring of 1863, housewives rioted and looted in the cities. On March 18, wives of soldiers robbed Atlanta stores. A vigilance committee formed at the city hall in August 1863 to slow further depreciation of Confederate currency by preventing persons from selling out their property and fleeing to the Federal lines. Later in the war, a writer to a newspaper complained that the some two thousand jobs the war brought to Atlanta's women too often went first to the wealthy families and not to the city's hundreds of needy women. A female Yankee wrote:

> *Many a woman walks eight or ten miles to town to get sewing; they often have no shoes, or only those made of cloth "pitched within & without"—and rarely ever wear stockings—for the simple reason they have none. The dresses of these country women are sometimes made of flour sacks dyed with bark; gingham "Sunbonnets" were long ago dispensed with—and those made of straw or the long leaved pine take their place…They said their rich neighbors persuaded their husbands to volunteer in the first of the war, promising that their families should never suffer. But the promise was forgotten, & the little sewing they could get hardly kept them alive.*

When the women of the Atlanta Hospital Association tried to sell sugar to finance an "invalid ladies" home, the Confederate army impressed that too.

Atlanta's hotels, "never anything to brag about," according to at least one critic, symbolized the decline of the city and the Southern nation. As the war continued, they no longer had sheets, towels or soap, all of which the soldiers had taken. Meals consisted of bacon and corn bread with rye substituted for coffee. The cost of room and board, however, soared to between thirty and forty dollars per day.

Eventually, more than 200 destitute Atlanta families of soldiers received relief from the State of Georgia, and a quarter of Atlanta's city budget went to helping the destitute and wounded soldiers, even beyond the considerable donations from private sources. Overall, the state had 84,119 "war indigents" by 1864, one-seventh of its total white population in 1860. At the war's end, Atlanta alone reportedly had more than 8,000 impoverished civilians, while the end of the war left Georgia with 36,000 more women, many of them destitute, than men.

Amidst these other problems, the population of the Gate City had security concerns that frequently went to blind panic and would have fueled paranoia were it not for the final fate of the city. By April 1862, officials had arrested three suspected enemy agents, two of whom they released for lack of evidence, although the men later went back into custody in Alabama. The third man went as a prisoner to Richmond with evidence of some sort of a sinister conspiracy. Richmond, shortly afterward, received reports that Yankees had taken over Atlanta on May 12 and, with the help of self-emancipated slaves, had started a riot and now sought to burn the city to the ground. Commander of the District of Georgia Brigadier General Alexander R. Lawton ordered Atlanta colonel George W. Lee to return to Atlanta from Savannah with local soldiers from the Thirty-eighth Georgia, to take command of the city and restore order.

Arriving by train with four companies, Lee found that the panic proved unwarranted. One warehouse had burned and, in doing so, had set afire some adjoining structures, all likely an accident caused by boys smoking cigars on the roof earlier in the day. The city frequently had such fires. Its *Daily Intelligencer* reported three fires in that same week, all believed to have been the result of carelessness.

Lee did find a city in fear. Atlanta and environs, north Georgia and the Western & Atlantic Railroad all had known and outspoken supporters of the Union and enemies of the Confederacy. Federal armies prepared to advance on Chattanooga, from where they could begin a campaign to take Atlanta.

Wilbur Kurtz's painting of the General being pursued by the Texas at the Great Locomotive Chase Memorial in Kennesaw, Georgia. *Courtesy the author.*

On April 12, twenty saboteurs, chiefly Ohio soldiers disguised as Southerners, under civilian James J. Andrews, seized the locomotive General and some boxcars at Big Shanty (the modern town of Kennesaw). They set out with a plan to burn the railroad's bridges in order to sever the one remaining rail connection between the Confederate states and its armies in Tennessee as the Federal army marched on Chattanooga and Huntsville.

Atlanta conductor William A. Fuller and shop foreman Anthony Murphy pursued the "engine thieves" on foot, by push car and, finally, with the engine Texas. The latter, under engineer Peter James Bracken, traveled in reverse until Andrews and his men, out of wood and water, abandoned the General north of Ringgold, Georgia, to flee into the woods. The fact that they fled on what happened to be a statewide militia muster day ensured their capture. Even their two comrades who had missed the day's adventure by oversleeping found themselves under arrest. Fuller, with no small amount of self-promotion, became the great hero in stopping the Andrews Raid through his Great Locomotive Chase.

The locomotive Texas today in the cyclorama building, Grant Park, Atlanta. *Courtesy Gus Welborn.*

In fact, James J. Andrews, a shadowy character from Kentucky who had worked for both sides as a spy, had made a number of major mistakes. His group, and any Union sympathizers helping them in Kennesaw, failed to provide anything like the needed incendiaries, tools and weapons. They had even forgotten to wake two of their comrades who had overslept. Any real planning made for the raid neglected to consider the incessant needs of the General for water and wood, and Andrews chose not to try to ambush even the seven men who pursued them on the Texas. The rain-soaked railroad bridges faced little real danger, and Chattanooga would remain in Confederate control until September 9, 1863.

A court-martial in Knoxville sentenced Andrews and seven of his men to death. Green J. Foreacre, then a provost marshal, hanged James J. Andrews on June 7 at the corner of Atlanta's Decatur and Peachtree Streets. Eleven days later, William Campbell, Samuel Robertson, Marion A. Ross, John Scott, Perry G. Shadrach, Samuel Slavens and George D. Wilson went to the gallows at Oakland Cemetery. Due to the intercession of Foreacre's successor, George W. Lee, no more of the raiders hanged. Eight of the prisoners eventually escaped, and Confederate authorities exchanged the other four. Nineteen soldiers of the raider party, living and dead, became the first recipients of the Medal of Honor. On April 25, 1866, the bodies of the group of seven executed raiders received reburial at the National Cemetery in Chattanooga. In 1887, a body removed from the alleged site of Andrews's grave joined them, but that may have been a misidentification; the mercenary spy and saboteur whose real name and background remains questionable may still lie today somewhere near Juniper and Third Streets.

The escape of the Andrews Raiders from Fulton County Jail. *From Pittenger,* Daring and Suffering.

These realities fueled reports of Yankee sympathizers, spies and incendiaries operating in Atlanta. Some of the city's residents supported the Union out of genuine patriotism, especially but not always from the community of native Yankees. They acted openly enough that the Confederate authorities knew their identities, although they did smuggle money and food to the Union soldiers held as prisoners in an old slave pen. Reports would appear after the city fell to Sherman of how those people also helped to hide Union soldiers, often by disguising them as Confederate wounded.

The public believed that Federal spies and saboteurs also walked among them. They even mistakenly believed that some of the Andrews Raiders still hid among the general population. Cornelius Hanleiter believed that spies used Atlanta's many railroad connections to communicate with their associates. Federal reports document agents of the United States Army passing in and out of the city throughout the war. Confederate officials in Atlanta arrested Mrs. E.F. Carter as a spy in January 1863. Lieutenant Harry Buford, also arrested as a spy in the Gate City, turned out to be Alice Williams of Mississippi. Richmond authorities ordered her returned to military service, but as a captain and chief of spies on the staff of Confederate general A.P. Stewart. She so converted to the Southern cause that she divorced her husband in the Union army and married a Georgian in order to become Jeruth DeCaulp.

Stories appeared in newspapers across the country that a man arrested in Atlanta claimed to be a major general in command of ten thousand slave volunteers in east Georgia. He allegedly plotted to take his secret army to the Gate City, after it fell to Union major general William S. Rosecrans, in order to acquire the arms for a systematic campaign of rapine and murder across the state. Officials in Hancock County investigated and found that this conspiracy actually consisted of only a few dozen slave artisans who would meet secretly at night to drink wine, occasionally drill and talk of emancipation. After they shot at a planter, thirty of their number suffered arrest and whippings. Two of their ringleaders went to the gallows.

The presence of so many newcomers encouraged belief in the most incredible of tales. Atlanta had always had a large transient and nonnative population, but the advance of the Federal armies in north Alabama and Tennessee, as well as the threat of invasion of Savannah and the Georgia coast, created a refugee problem. The city's population grew to over fifteen thousand, and later to twenty-two thousand, the majority of whom came to the city as strangers since 1860, including Southern sympathizers from Kentucky. In May 1861, a local newspaper asked how many spies and arsonists hid among the city's newly arrived beggars and strangers. Georgia governor Joseph E. Brown ended, for a time, the shipments of cotton on the state railroad because collecting it in railheads like Atlanta left the bales vulnerable to theft or use as fuel to start fires.

The city's new citizens also included speculators who sought to make fortunes in cotton, gold, bank notes, bread and meat. George W. Lee wrote:

> [Atlanta] *has been since the Commencement of the revolution—a point of rendezvous of traitors, Swindlers, extortioners* [sic], *and Counterfeiters. The population as a predominant element is a mixture of Jews, New England Yankees, and of refugees shirking military duties.*

On a more positive note, the refugees also brought their newspapers. The *Chattanooga Rebel*, *Knoxville Register* and *Memphis Daily Appeal* would all come to call Atlanta home, in addition to the city's four regular dailies and various journals. The Federal advance had forced the *Appeal* from Memphis, Grenada, Jackson and Selma, but on July 22, 1864, it would be the last newspaper to leave Civil War Atlanta. Before then, and as the *Atlanta Appeal*, it supplied news to its readers and the Yankee press, through copies of the paper found on dead Confederate soldiers (General Sherman was an avid reader of the *Appeal*), with the story of the last days of the doomed city. Its historian would write of its staff—John Reid McClanahan, Carolina Dill and Benjamin F. Dill—"Their scrappy backgrounds enabled them to exasperate and out wit generals. Ulysses S. Grant, William T. Sherman and James H. Wilson chased them across four states, yet they could not silence the 'Voice of the Confederacy.'" (The paper later moved to Macon and Columbus before returning, finally, to Memphis after the war.)

In April 1862, the press had much to report. Contrary to claims made by Lee's critics, he did not declare martial law. He did make Atlanta into a formal military post and took command of the hospitals, the quartermaster stores, conscripts and seemingly all other aspects of the Confederate government establishment, including more than $60 million worth of government stores. To restore public confidence, he issued a string of orders for the arrest of any soldier or civilian found without a pass, as well as to incarcerate any slave or free person of color out after the legally imposed curfew of 9:00 p.m. without a pass or an owner. Whatever he felt about race, he enforced existing laws and drew criticism for being too liberal in providing passes to the city's black population.

The city government, in its concerns for security, acted with less tact in its treatment of slaves and freedmen. It further restricted their movements beyond Georgia's already stringent slave codes. Black Atlantans often appeared before the mayor's court for using offensive language to a white person. The standard punishment consisted of thirty-nine lashes on the bare back for insolence. Atlanta and Confederate officials prevented the sale of liquor to slaves. They also tightly regulated the renting of horses and carriages to slaves in order to prevent their escape or meeting to conspire in a slave uprising. Atlanta police supervised the Negro balls held for raising money for the families of soldiers and for servants who had gone to war with their masters, but the city council even outlawed those in 1863 as a public nuisance and a security risk.

Colonel George W. Lee and his men soon had to return the security of Atlanta to the city's twenty-man police force and its three-thousand-man (draft exempt) volunteer fire companies. Also counted as local defense companies, the fire companies put on a good parade, with bright armor, banners flying and marital music. Lee had orders to return to Savannah, where the usual mismanagement of the military had made him senior officer of the regiments there. He had to move as many men as he could, as quickly as possible, to Virginia to help in blocking new Federal offensives. The colonel succeeded in getting almost a division to Richmond before a recurrence of his tuberculosis forced him to resign in early July 1862.

By the end of the month, however, Lee accepted the position of garrison commander and provost marshal in Atlanta at the rank of captain. Lee would form a Provost Guard Battalion and employ detectives such as George McGinnely, proprietor of the Trout House hotel, for he could read character and knew everyone. James Gettys McGready Ramsey from Knoxville, Tennessee, and Captain James A. Burton from west of the Mississippi River also came to Atlanta to work as detectives. The latter would, while in Georgia, arrest a Yankee spy, an extortionist, a forger of passports, a forger of army papers, a forger of all types, four deserters and a man who took money under false pretenses.

All Confederate provost marshals found enforcing the prohibitions on alcohol to be their greatest problem. Cornelius Hanleiter wrote in his diary of finding "split scull," "rifle," "knock knee," "O.B. Joyful," "knock in the head," "sure shot" and "rot gut" widely available in Atlanta. The problems from this substance abuse included violence, theft and damage to property. Much of the whiskey proved to have been diluted with toxic ingredients as cheap fillers. The result, one Atlantan wrote, came in two varieties, one of which tasted like swallowing a cat and the other like pulling it back out by the tail. Joseph Harford, for example, found himself arrested six or seven times for operating a small dram shop and for selling to soldiers, Irishmen, slaves and anyone else what Lee, a former saloon owner, described as "his miserable poisonous concoction which he has been in the habit of calling Spirits." Harford usually concealed his product in a carpet sack, but he also brought it into the city in barrels, nailed and secreted it among other goods, as he "endeavored in a thousand ways to evade the law." Governor Brown received reports, especially from drought-stricken north Georgia, that farmers refused to sell corn to starving families, even those of soldiers, because more money came from illegally producing and then selling whiskey to soldiers than from feeding hungry people.

Lee banned the sale of alcohol to members of the military and ordered the arrest of anyone found drunk in the streets. He later extended these orders to outlying areas, where troops had been stationed. The Provost Guard busted whiskey barrels and emptied wagonloads of alcohol into the streets. The home-brew continued to come in, however, and often under the pretense of supplying the city's Confederate hospitals. The whiskey, more often, found itself on sale to soldiers at railroad stations.

Many of Atlanta's most dubious characters, including among the so-called secret Yankees, and their lawyers fought back. Government officials and politicians also took bribes, used influence or took retaliation upon persons who enforced the vague prohibition laws. Lee, for example, took a risk when he "washed" Peachtree Street with the "spiritual" T.O. Kyle's twelve barrels of whiskey as Kyle's brother sat on the city council. Even Colonel Marvel J. Camden of Chattanooga used his position as manager of the State of Georgia's Western & Atlantic Railroad to smuggle whiskey into Atlanta. Governor Brown ordered the government to purchase Camden's whiskey or to send it back to Camden at Camden's expense. When the governor eased the restrictions on whiskey production, officially to supply the military hospitals in Richmond, he discovered that he had facilitated a whiskey ring that took in $120,000 in profits. A woman named Harrington in Augusta shipped whiskey to her sister, another war widow in Atlanta, allegedly for the hospitals. The provost marshal believed that they lied, but he still paid for the alcohol and had it turned over to the medical department. General John K. Jackson ordered an end to the campaign against alcohol in Atlanta only for his superior, General Braxton Bragg, to restore it when Bragg proclaimed martial law in the city in 1863.

Conspiracy and fraud existed in many forms in Civil War Atlanta. A man named George from Athens, Georgia, conned his way into the highest circles of the Confederate government in Richmond with just an officer's uniform. Lee had him arrested twice in Atlanta and sent both times to General Braxton Bragg's headquarters. Each time, "Gentleman George" conned the general into letting him go. The city early became a center for the army's endless need for shoes. A local quartermaster ordered footwear from the shops set up in the state penitentiary in Milledgeville but then rejected them only as a means of profitably selling the same shoes to the public in Atlanta. Similarly, a group of soldiers was caught selling five wagonloads of military supplies, worth between $60,000 and $75,000, just outside of the city.

A "Jacobin Club," Lee called it, or a group that claimed political motives for its private criminal activities, has been made to appear in some recent publications as a club of oppressed heroes rather than one full of opportunists. These "secret Yankees," as sympathetic modern writers dub them, would weave exaggerated tales of a Confederate reign of terror that, when analyzed in light of the facts and their own statements, comes across as an insult to the sufferings of real patriots throughout history. The real "secret Yankees" attempted to make money from the war, including smuggling local cotton to New York through ports in Florida. Several Atlanta companies operated legal (to the Confederate States of America) blockade runners—ships that slipped past the Federal warships that blocked the South's few ports. Richard Peters, for example, formed a partnership that made $3 million blockade running. The "secret Yankees" of Atlanta smuggled into the Confederacy necessities that they then sold to desperate people at the highest prices possible. They went so far as to violate the laws of both warring nations.

Many of these same smugglers and speculators also held important and profitable posts in the Confederate government. William O. Markham, a former Atlanta mayor, for example, would claim that the Confederate officials forced him to sell his interest in the Atlanta Rolling Mill to the government and that he only did extensive business with the Confederacy because of extreme pressure placed on him by George W. Lee, the Confederate provost marshal. Markham did rent an office to Lee and also had the provost marshal successfully sued for harassment in the local Confederate court. After the war, he would unsuccessfully petition the United States government for compensation for property he lost to the Federal siege of Atlanta. Similarly, successful businessman and nominal slave barber Robert Webster became notorious for speculating in currency, and he helped a Federal colonel to escape. He only spent a short time in jail, however, and would later serve in a citizen's delegation that accompanied Mayor Calhoun when he surrendered Atlanta to Sherman. The most celebrated case of a member of this Jacobin Club being harassed involved successful Irish dry goods merchant Michael Myers. His critics claimed that he refused to accept Confederate currency, passed counterfeit bills and illegally sold liquor. (The bootlegger Joseph Harford would write his eulogy.) Friends of Myers accused Confederate officials of beating him to death with a rifle butt while in custody. An autopsy determined that he had a stroke and actually died at home, while under medical care, from natural causes brought about by his notorious alcoholism.

Government officials held trials for six outspoken white Atlanta Unionists suspected of treasonable activities, including espionage, but all of the defendants obtained release. Captain George W. Lee had other people detained and interrogated, including Cyrena Stone, an avowed Union sympathizer whose modern biographer believes aided escaped slaves, Federal prisoners of war and spies. Her husband, Amherst W. Stone, a Northerner and lawyer who operated a successful law practice helping the Confederate government to sequester the property of other Unionists, would later suffer arrest and imprisonment in the North for his role in the cotton smuggling plot. The inquisition of Cyrena, however, consisted only of a polite, brief public questioning, not under oath, by Lee about Unionist meetings and an alleged plot of three hundred Atlanta Union sympathizers to organize a slave uprising. She only complained that she "saw" in all of Lee's features a hatred of Yankees. By early 1863, the Confederate government ended his investigations and had his prisoners released.

The war brought the city other threats in an age when any financial institution, as well as any government, could issue paper money. Jabez Richards discovered $1,200 in counterfeit currency in his store's receipts. By November, fear of bogus bills caused even Atlanta's *Southern Confederacy* to publish a list of the only bank notes that it would accept as payment. The Confederate secretary of the treasury placed George W. Lee in charge of finding and stopping this trade, for Atlanta and for the whole South. He created a small detective force, what amounted to his version of the later United States Secret Service, which included G.H. Gilbert. The latter worked undercover in Atlanta, Chattanooga and southwest Georgia. His investigations found few counterfeit money notes among innocent civilians, although considerable amounts of them turned up in the possession of captured Yankee soldiers. As the United States government refused to recognize the Confederate States of America, printers behind the Union lines could legally print Confederate notes that often were of better quality than the official issue of the Southern nation. Lee had at least two persons caught with bogus notes under lock and key by 1863. One of these prisoners escaped but soon found himself back in custody. He had tried to befriend the young son of Dr. Stephen T. Biggors, but the boy helped to set a trap for the man that resulted in the miscreant being arrested.

IV

The Siege

More than 110,000 men with 254 cannons from three Federal armies named for the Cumberland, Ohio and Tennessee Rivers prepared in the spring of 1864 to march on Atlanta. They faced the 55,000 to 75,000 men and 144 heavy guns of the Confederate armies named for the states of Mississippi and Tennessee, as well as the state and militia forces mustered by Georgia governor Joseph E. Brown, in one of the most incredible military campaigns in history.

Fought over a vast area of widely varying landscape, the campaign could have gone any number of ways based on personalities, weather, disease, luck and other factors. Despite the differences in numbers, the weapons of the age gave special strategic and tactical advantages to the defender, as would be demonstrated across the Confederate States of America in 1864 in piles of the dead. The Federal advance into north Georgia of the previous autumn had ended with a stunning Confederate victory at Chickamauga on September 19–20, 1863. Yet Americans would again march, fight, suffer and die for control of a railroad city not twenty years old, the occupation of which many observers believed, at the time, would decide the fate of nations.

Few aspects of the Civil War have more widely accepted—and published—myths and misunderstandings, however, than the story of the fall of Atlanta to the Federal forces of General William Tecumseh Sherman. Atlanta was not, for example, the single great indispensable munitions, manufacturing or even transportation center of the Confederacy. Augusta, Charleston, Columbus (Georgia), Columbus (Mississippi), Macon,

Memphis, Mobile, Montgomery, New Orleans, Richmond and Selma all had significant operations with secondary works in such towns as Athens (Georgia), Albany, Dalton and Rome that together contributed in major ways to supplying the Confederate military. Atlanta's arsenal made a significant contribution to the Southern cause, but it hardly challenged Richmond in that regard. In November 1862, for example, the Atlanta Arsenal came in third in small arms ammunition behind Richmond and Augusta, respectively, and tied for second (Richmond again came in first) with Augusta and Columbus (Mississippi) in rounds of field artillery ammunition. The armory, arsenal, laboratory and other manufactories in Confederate Macon alone provided everything that an army needed, from matches to artillery. Those works, and those of Augusta, rearmed the Army of Tennessee after its disasters in 1863 and 1864.

General Sherman, at center leaning on cannon, with officers in Atlanta. *Courtesy Library of Congress.*

Atlanta only served as a critical transportation center as long as supplies passed through and were sent from it to the Confederate forces in Tennessee via the Western & Atlantic Railroad. As half of the Confederate army's pork and a large part of its beef came from Tennessee, some question exists as to how often those necessities passed from or to Atlanta. Beef later had to come from Florida through the Gate City. When Chattanooga fell to Federal forces, that same track and its long tunnel became a threat to the Confederacy because it then became the critical supply line for Union armies moving on Atlanta and beyond. Even after the Gate City fell to Sherman, Jefferson Davis rode other Confederate railroads from Richmond to Lovejoy, hardly more than twenty miles from Federal-occupied Atlanta, to plead with the Southern people to send back to his army their men who had deserted. He proclaimed that the war had not yet been lost, despite the surrender of the Gate City. Confederate commanding general Joseph E. Johnston saw defending Atlanta as necessary, at least in order to prevent the release of tens of thousands of desperate Federal prisoners of war at Andersonville Prison in deep southwest Georgia. He, Robert E. Lee and many other leaders, North and South, believed that the survival of the South's armies trumped keeping Atlanta. Sherman's orders only called for the destruction of the Confederate Army of Tennessee.

Capturing Atlanta, however, as the Union general saw it, would mean that his armies had finally opened a gate to the empty shell that remained of the dying Confederate States of America. The Southern nation had shrunk to the point that it had finally become sustainable, with viable internal lines of communication. Southern plans for victory lay in holding off the Federal military from Atlanta, Charleston, Mobile and Richmond to have a chance at winning independence through the presidential election of November 1864. To dash even those hopes, General Grant planned coordinated simultaneous strategic assaults on what remained of the Confederate nation from different directions so as to stretch out its dwindling military forces to face annihilation from overwhelming numbers of Union soldiers.

All of these campaigns ultimately failed in the spring and summer of 1864, except for the Atlanta Campaign, and at terrible losses in lives of soldiers. Had the battles for the city gone against Sherman, the defeats would likely have had only limited political repercussions, especially in light of the tens of thousands of Federal dead in Grant's failed campaign to take Richmond. The Lincoln administration would have won the all-important electoral vote and reelection even if the fall of the Gate City had not also guaranteed it a popular mandate in November 1864. George B. McClellan, the Democratic nominee, was committed to restoring the Union, although had he won election, he would have tried to continue the war without a popular mandate or even the support of his party.

William Tecumseh Sherman, a visionary, inspired and eccentric commander to the point that some modern researchers diagnose him as being bipolar, had vast advantages in numbers and supplies for his campaign to take Atlanta. He had the confidence of his superiors, the high morale of veteran soldiers and near perfect weather. His subordinate commanders served him well. The highly successful Virginia-born Major General George H. Thomas commanded the Army of the Cumberland (Fourth, Fourteenth and Twentieth Corps, plus cavalry), more than half of Sherman's soldiers, and handled all of the campaign's staff functions. His subordinates included veterans Major Generals O.O. Howard and Joseph Hooker. Major General James B. McPherson commanded the Army of the Tennessee with its Fifteenth Corps (Major General John A. Logan) and the Sixteenth Corps (Major General Grenville M. Dodge). The Army of the Ohio, Major General John M. Schofield commanding, consisted for the campaign of Twenty-third Corps and Major George Stoneman's cavalry.

Opposing this well-led, supplied and organized veteran war machine would be General Joseph E. Johnston and the Confederate armies of Tennessee and Mississippi. His three corps had as commanders veteran Lieutenant Generals Leonidas J. Polk, William J. Hardee and John B. Hood. Major General Joseph Wheeler and Brigadier General William H. Jackson commanded the cavalry. With Georgia state troops and militia under Major General Gustavus W. Smith, the force opposing Sherman was made up of men of widely varying military experience and equipment.

Johnston had already lost the confidence of President Jefferson Davis and Georgia governor Joseph E. Brown, a situation made worse by letters from Hardee and Hood that undermined him to Davis. His subordinate commanders had a deserved reputation of being contentious. No one used the word "brilliant" to describe any of the men commanding his corps, although some of the division commanders would rise to corps command by the end of campaign and become legends of the war. General morale in the western army had suffered in years past from the poor treatment of the common soldiers and the belief that often they had been ordered to sacrifice their lives needlessly.

Sherman began the campaign on May 7, 1864, with a movement against Dalton, the largest town in Georgia north of Atlanta, in order to seize the Western & Atlantic Railroad. The weeks of maneuver that followed concentrated on seizing those tracks, both to supply his army from the north and to cut off its use from the south for his opponents. Sherman's army would need one hundred boxcars of supplies per day for its campaign. Eventually, he would assign as much as half of his army to the Department of the Etowah, his organization for protecting those tracks from often-effective raids by local guerillas and the Confederate army. Tunnel Hill, north of Dalton, fell to the Union advance, as did Snake Creek Gap fifteen miles to the south. General Johnston withdrew to the south and then blocked the Federal attempt to cut the railroad at Resaca on May 14 and 15. Major General McPherson's Army of the Tennessee then maneuvered around the Confederate position, forcing Johnston's corps to withdraw to Cassville. The Southern general set a trap that failed due to conflict among his corps commanders. Constant movements and fighting from May 7 to June 4 at Rocky Face Ridge, Resaca, New Hope Church and Pickett's Mill (all minor Confederate defensive victories) finally brought the two opposing forces farther south to Kennesaw Mountain, then within sight of Atlanta. From June 5 to July 3, fighting went on along a ten-mile stretch of lines. On June 27, Sherman hurled his legions against entrenched Confederate troops. The Southern soldiers turned back the assaults at a cost of some three thousand lost to Sherman's armies and seven hundred to the defenders. Confederate lieutenant general and Episcopal bishop Leonidas Polk died from artillery fire on June 14, however. The citizens of Atlanta gave

The Battle of Kennesaw Mountain. *From* Battles and Leaders of the Civil War.

him a memorial service. For all but the opening of the battle, the casualty ratio ran ten to one against the Federals.

Schofield's Twenty-third Corps, however, moved around the Confederate lines to push the campaign farther south to the Chattahoochee River. Johnston had thirty-six arrow-shaped forts, called "Shoupades" after their inventor, Brigadier General Francis A. Shoup, to try again to block the Federal advance. Slaves built these works and Atlanta's other defenses, as they had the antebellum city. African Americans also served and died in the somewhat integrated Confederate army to a degree only now beginning to be understood. Sherman, however, marched on Atlanta without black troops or wanting any, regarding freedmen as incapable of soldiering. When asked if they could not stop a bullet as well as anyone, the general famously responded yes, but a sandbag worked better. He mistakenly believed that he had no African American soldiers in his army except in the labor battalions.

Sherman succeeded in flanking the fortifications on the Chattahoochee without conflict by crossing north of Peachtree Creek. The shallowness of the river and the fact that the campaign had reduced the Southern army's strength by one-third had forced Johnston to spread his forces so thin that, in at least one place, only a few men and a bridge stood between the Federal army and Atlanta. Confederate general Samuel French had observed both armies from the heights above the Kennesaw battlefields. He would remember the extreme activity in the Union army, with wagons, ambulances, tents, cavalry and infantry as far as he could see. Nothing seemed to move in what he saw of his own lines, just an occasional piece of canvas among the trees.

Brigadier General Kenner Garrards's Union cavalry occupied Roswell and destroyed its textile factories. (The National Park Service supervises the ruins today. Roswell, however, has several mansions still standing that date from before the war.) The French manager failed to persuade the general that French nationals actually owned the property, even if it obviously made blankets for the Southern army. Other Federal troops destroyed the New Manchester mills. (The ruins of those mills are today part of Sweetwater Creek State Park near Lithia Springs.) General Sherman subsequently declared the some seven hundred textile workers, most of whom were women, guilty of treason and had hundreds of them, along with their children, shipped north of the Ohio River to keep them from further serving the Confederacy. In Marietta, Union soldiers allegedly raped some of the women being held there as prisoners. Most of these civilians never found the means to return home. They became the basis of the Civil War legend of the "Roswell Women."

The Federal corps now advanced on Atlanta with Thomas's Army of the Cumberland closing in from the North; McPherson's Army of the Tennessee, reinforced with Major General Frank P. Blair's Seventeenth Corps, from Decatur and the east; and Schofield's Twenty-third Corps filling the gap from the northeast. Initially, the invaders camped along the north side of Peachtree Creek on the very ground where the settlement of what became Atlanta had begun hardly more than a generation earlier.

Construction of defenses around Atlanta to meet such a threat had begun in the summer of 1863, when the fall of Vicksburg compelled the Confederate government to begin fortifying its remaining cities. Maine-born Lemuel P. Grant, who had come to the Gate City to build and manage its railroads, now set out to defend his new home as a captain of Confederate engineers. The Confederate government hired and impressed slaves from nearby counties. By October 30, 1863, Grant had encircled the city with twelve miles of trenches, rifle pits, gun emplacements and forts. He had seventeen redoubts erected, each connected by trenches that allowed for the addition of abatis, palisades, chevaux-de-frise or other barricades as obstacles to prevent attackers from reaching the slopes of the forts and the gun emplacements. (Today, all that survives of his fortifications is Fort Walker in Grant Park.) Wood from buildings in the potential line of fire went into building the fortifications. Sherman's forces never breached those lines, but Confederate General Hood, in the midst of the coming fighting, would criticize these defenses as too close to the city and for not better protecting the west side of Atlanta. His soldiers, however, improved the trenches based on hard-earned experiences at Chattanooga and Kennesaw Mountain.

These fortifications became only the most obvious sign of the coming crisis. On May 18, 1864, Governor Joseph Brown called out the state militia, and five days later Atlanta mayor James Calhoun ordered all able-bodied civilian men to meet at city hall to serve in the home defense companies. He insisted that any man who declined to come should leave the city.

Aside from the army, Atlanta's population tripled to more than twenty-two thousand people, largely consisting of desperate refugees, including orphans, runaways and vagabonds, black and white—what humorist Henry "Bill Arp" Smith, one of their number, called "runagees." Citizens complained of the smells downtown from the slaughterhouses, hospitals and stables created by the war. Everywhere filth and garbage overflowed. The constant passage of steam locomotives filled the compact city with smoke and noise. Five Points, in the center of the city, became infamous for its brothels, gambling dens and saloons, set up to accommodate the soldiers. Citizens blamed the army and

This page and previous: Some of the Confederate fortifications around Atlanta. *Courtesy Library of Congress*

the refugees for increased thefts, but everyone complained of the high prices in the city. With the advance of the Federal corps almost to Lemuel Grant's line of defense, many people who could fled south from the beleaguered city on the Macon & Western Railroad, soon to be the only exit. Other Atlantans reached the Federal lines for transportation north to Tennessee and beyond. Mayor Calhoun, an early opponent of immediate secession, stayed to serve his city, as did its often-criticized fire battalion.

President Davis, fearing for the safety of Atlanta, began to consider replacing Johnston. Robert E. Lee and other persons whose advice the president sought argued for keeping him in command of the army of Tennessee but abandoning Atlanta. Davis finally replaced Johnston with acting general John B. Hood on July 17. Hood and the other corps commanders immediately but unsuccessfully petitioned to keep Johnston in command until Atlanta's fate had been decided. No one in the army defending Atlanta seemed happy to see the change in command. Hood had lost the use of an arm at Gettysburg and a leg at Chickamauga, but he had a deserved reputation for winning critical battles by personally leading desperate charges at the cost of high casualties. He now determined to turn back the Federal advance by going on the offensive to win, as he usually did, by courage and luck rather than command skill.

The first assault occurred at Peachtree Creek, north of Atlanta, on July 20, 1864. Hood hurled two of his three corps against Thomas's three corps of the Army of the Cumberland, with the intention of destroying them before throwing his entire army, from the west, against the rest of Sherman's forces. When the attack commenced at 4:00 p.m., Thomas was carrying out Sherman's orders to cross Peachtree Creek and proceed south toward Atlanta.

Confusion and miscommunication in the execution of a complicated plan resulted in a Confederate defeat that could have ended the campaign for Atlanta with a Union triumph that afternoon. Thomas's Federals quickly responded to Hood's assault, fought along Collier Road, and drove off the gray-clad soldiers. At the same time, McPherson advanced the Union's Army of the Tennessee to within two and a half miles of the center of the weakly guarded city. Fearing attack and cautious by nature, McPherson chose not to move farther. He had the DeGress battery begin shelling the city, hitting two buildings and killing a girl on Ivy and East Ellis Streets with the first shots. The day ended with Sherman suffering some seventeen hundred casualties, but nearly taking Atlanta, to Hood's likely twenty-five hundred men lost. The next day would be one of horror as the hospitals of both armies worked feverishly to save lives. More shells rained on the city, as one by one buildings took hits. The few thousand people remaining in Atlanta lost hope. Soldiers on both sides expected continued hard fighting.

Hood fulfilled their fears on the next day, July 22, when he sent Hardee's Corps and Wheeler's cavalry to turn McPherson's reportedly unguarded flank, silence the Federal batteries and capture McPherson's wagon train in Decatur. If the Federal line began to crumble, Cheatham's Corps would join in the battle while Stewart's Corps kept Thomas's Army of the Cumberland from coming to the rescue. Troops moved out of the trenches to assemble at Five Points before moving to the attack.

The civilians and the nearby Union army mistakenly believed that Hood's army was evacuating the city. Some straggling soldiers, women in the sex trade and other Atlantans believed the rumor enough to begin plundering stores and saloons. As Hood's regiments marched to battle, the thieves left the city with wagonloads of loot.

The subsequent battle on Bald Hill, known as the Battle of Atlanta partly because of the popularity of the cyclorama that would commemorate it, became another disaster for Hood. As with the fighting on Peachtree Creek, historian Albert Castel wrote that the Confederates made their assault "in a disorganized, pell-mell, virtually blind fashion." Manigault's Alabamians, Mississippians and South Carolinians temporarily captured the four guns of the DeGress battery before, for reasons never explained, receiving orders for their withdrawal. When the fighting along what would one day be Memorial Drive north along Moreland Avenue to the Carter Center ended, the Federal Army of the Tennessee had lost 3,722 men, as well as twenty-two pieces of artillery and five stands of flags, to Hood's estimated 5,500 casualties. Major General James M. McPherson (for whom the nearby Fort McPherson would one day be named) and Confederate major general W.H.T. Walker lay among the dead. Had Sherman ordered it, Thomas could have led his Army of the Cumberland into the city from the north almost unopposed.

Whereas Peachtree Creek had brought the sound of war to Atlanta, the city had become a battlefield itself on July 22. Hood watched the battle from the second floor of a house next to Oakland Cemetery. Soldiers, wagons and horses crowded the streets. Shells fell into Atlanta from the battle. The long trains of ambulances brought in the wounded, North and South, to State Square. These men spent little or no time in the city's military hospitals, however, but instead joined the other sick and wounded who had been evacuated south since July 6. A truce allowed for the burial of the dead on the battlefield—for piles of unknown Confederate dead, graves amounted to shallow pits.

Many of the remaining Atlantans had stories of the battle, but the Clayton family's experiences proved exceptional. William Wirt Clayton had stayed in Atlanta with most of his large family because some of his daughters were sick with typhus, which they had probably contracted from working as volunteers in the military hospitals. While he and his wife worried over their children, Confederate regiments marched outside the windows of the house on the night of July 21. Their daughter Gussie died the next day, but the shelling prevented her burial in Oakland Cemetery. Neighbors, some of them Unionists (the Claytons were Confederates), such as former mayor William Markham, risked their lives to obtain a coffin, but because of the fighting, the Claytons and their friends had to bury Gussie in their garden as shells fell around them. (The Claytons had Gussie reinterred in their family plot in Oakland years later.)

Sherman considered a direct assault on the north and east side of Atlanta but then heard persuasive arguments that the strength of the enemy trenches would make attacks on Atlanta into the Battle of Kennesaw Mountain all over again. Instead, the general ordered his cavalry to go on a raid south to cut the city's last railroad while his Army of the Tennessee passed to the west side of the city. Hood learned of the movement and attempted to assault the Federal columns at Ezra Church, around today's Mozley Park and Westview Cemetery, on July 28. The resulting battle accomplished nothing more than adding 632 casualties to Sherman's rolls while Hood's losses came to close to 3,000 men. Again, the Union command considered a rush into the city, only to settle for the victory at hand. Major General Joseph Wheeler's horsemen pursued Sherman's raiders and wrecked two-thirds of the Federal cavalry while taking more than 1,000 prisoners in the process. Men who had planned to first cut the railroad to Atlanta and then to rescue Union prisoners of war in Macon and Andersonville failed in all parts of their mission. As with so much of the Atlanta campaign, success and failure ultimately rested on blind obsessive gambles.

Both armies also suffered such losses from sickness that, without fresh troops, the Atlanta Campaign could have ended when one side or the other essentially disappeared. During that summer, some one-third to one-fourth of the Federal army and one-third of the Confederate forces spent some time in hospitals. Especially when soldiers crowded in trenches, the creeks become foul with waste to make sickness and flies worse. Desertions and, in the Union army, expirations of service took a toll as well. The soldiers of the two opposing forces suffered from stress, boredom, random artillery shells, snipers, dysentery and the notorious effects of a summer in the Georgia woods, including ticks, mosquitoes, chiggers and snakes. Practical jokes, music, whiskey (when available), fraternizing with the enemy and letters from home could only go so far to relieve pressure. Union soldiers engaged in plunder, while their Confederate counterparts used any opportunity to escape.

Sherman, however, found the entrenchments around Atlanta still too formidable to storm, especially after he sent two corps in a failed effort to cut the city's last railroads through East Point by way of Utoy Creek. In August, both armies watched their respective supplies dwindle while the cavalry of each side went on failed raids to cut the other's respective railroad supply lines. The soldiers in both armies continued to believe that their side, respectively, had won the previous battles and would yet win the campaign.

General Sherman had finally come to see the bloody pointlessness of capturing Atlanta and considered abandoning the siege to devastate the countryside for miles around. At length, he chose to make the traditional mistake in a siege and add to his growing reputation as "the merchant of terror" by ordering an intensified bombardment, for day and night, on

Ephraim Ponder's plantation after the bombardment. *Courtesy Library of Congress.*

August 9. As late as 1994, construction crews still uncovered the unexploded shells that were fired from Federal batteries.

Atlanta still had in it between two thousand and five thousand civilians, fed by rations from the army and largely living in a refugee camp on the south side of the city. At the same time, soldiers destroyed scarce housing out of military necessity or just for fuel. Many of the city's poor had no means to leave and felt abandoned by their government, the speculators who had grown rich off the war and the wealthy. All of the buildings withstood the shelling, although many suffered too much damage to be habitable. Only one grocer remained open, and the city essentially ceased to function as more than a railroad-supplied prison. Ephraim Ponder's house, for example, took more than one hundred shells and absorbed more than a ton of shrapnel. The Clayton family, following the death of their youngest daughter, sought protection from the bombardment in the Georgia Railroad Bank building, where William W. Clayton had been an officer. A shell that landed in their home only frightened two slave girls living with them, but another narrowly missed Clayton's wife, Caroline, and landed, unexploded, in the house. A servant gently carried it out into the street. Civilians became adept at timing the crossing of streets, as well as at avoiding the most often shelled sections of the city and structures such as churches, because of the steeples rising above the trees. To avoid the shells, many Atlantans dug "bombproofs" (shelters) in their yards, but that gave thieves new opportunities to rob unguarded houses. Atlanta's fire companies had long drawn criticism as draft dodgers, but in July and August 1864, they earned praise as they courageously fought a desperate battle to put out the fires started by the barrage. The task proved too much for them, and the regular citizens had to pitch in to form bucket lines to put out fires, sometimes while in their nightclothes. Failure to remove bales of cotton by rail created huge fire hazards that threatened to destroy Atlanta with the great American staple that had built the city as a transportation center. Federal soldiers claimed that they could sometimes hear the cries and screams of women and children in the city during the thirty-six-day shelling.

On August 10, General Sherman ordered the Federal artillery to fire at will instead of in timed sequence. The change affected one of the Claytons' servants as he crossed the street with food for the sick children. At the sound of any shell, he would fall to the ground with his tray.

The Confederates answered the shelling with seven pieces of large siege artillery brought up by rail from Savannah, but Sherman added to his assault some Rodman guns from Chattanooga that fired thirty-three-pound projectiles. In the middle of August, a Union battery ended a few days of relative quiet. The

The Georgia Railroad Bank building that provided refuge to the Clayton family during the bombardment. *Courtesy Library of Congress.*

An Atlanta home and its bombproof. *Courtesy Library of Congress.*

Confederates responded with the fire of a siege gun on Peachtree Tree so large that it had required three days just to move it into place. Sherman, however, ordered his intensive artillery bombardment of almost five thousand shells on August 9. That day, ten Confederate and twelve Federal batteries exchanged fire with the city of Atlanta as collateral damage between them. At least seven of the some twenty casualties of the siege died instantly or were mortally wounded that day, including African American barber Solomon Luckie. The dead apparently counted only one Confederate soldier, an officer visiting a civilian who was

Atlantans in a bombproof. *From* Harper's Weekly.

mortally wounded with her little boy. The guns finally ceased fire, and the worst day of the siege in terms of damage and loss of life ended.

The barrage finally stopped on August 25 as Sherman's forces disappeared from the east side of Atlanta to begin new flanking maneuvers to cut off its last two railroads. His more numerous batteries than the Confederate gunners had an added advantage in that they had the buildings in a city for a target. This huge shelling, however, brought him no closer to capturing the city. Atlantans gathered in their damaged churches on August 28 to thank God for the end of the shelling. They also held a ball at the still standing Medical College building. Thousands of shells had entered the city, but contrary to press reports of hundreds of dead and wounded, historian Stephen Davis believes that only some twenty people died and between one hundred and two hundred people suffered wounds from the shelling. Dr. P.P. Noel D'Alvigny remembered doing 107 amputations at his makeshift hospital at the Medical College. The Claytons even brought their healthy daughters back to the city so that they could face the future together. When reunited, they escaped on one of the last trains to leave the doomed city. Many of the city's prominent citizens stayed to the end or nearly the end, and some of them, such as Samuel Richards and Mary Rawson, left detailed accounts of those dark days. Atlanta's remaining Unionists avoided the attention of the city's Confederates. A group of Mississippi soldiers threatened to destroy a store found to have a copy of the antislavery novel *Uncle Tom's Cabin*.

The last formal battle of the Atlanta Campaign began shortly after. On August 31, 1864, Hardee launched two Confederate corps against entrenched Federal troops just outside of Jonesboro in an elaborate plan to save his railroad supply line and to drive the Union divisions back across the Flint, if not the Chattahoochee, River. Hood even envisioned continuing on to destroy Sherman's supply base at Marietta.

The resulting two-day battle ended with predictable results and for the usual reasons, but for both armies. As always, Hood asked too much of his outnumbered, poorly led, barefoot and demoralized army. On the first day, Southern soldiers made poorly coordinated attacks into a sheer wall of carefully directed enemy fire. The Confederates lost at least 2,200 men to Federal losses of 172 casualties. Sherman's army at the same time cut the Macon & Western Railroad elsewhere while unintentionally splitting Hood's army in two. For one last time, Sherman lost an opportunity to capture the Gate City by force. He also could have destroyed the long-suffering Confederate Army of Tennessee.

Those opportunities, too, passed. Due to miscommunication, difficult terrain and long-distance mismanagement, Sherman ordered what became his own uncoordinated attacks on the second day of the Battle of Jonesboro (September 1) against the one remaining enemy (Hardee's) corps. The Union troops did break through the Confederate line and even captured two batteries, but Hardee and his men escaped in good order to join Stephen D. Lee's Corps at Lovejoy Station, as would their comrades in Atlanta. The Confederates did lose some 1,400 men, although that number likely included 900 deserters, at the second day of the fighting at Jonesboro compared to 1,273 Federal losses.

At that same moment, in Atlanta, the militia and most of Hood's remaining corps prepared to evacuate the city and escape south while slipping past Sherman's army. The post office closed, allegedly leaving more than 100,000 letters torn open for possible money and then scattered to the wind by retreating Confederates. Reportedly, paper covered ten miles of the Covington Road. The commissary opened its warehouses to civilians and soldiers alike, while the looting of private homes and businesses went unimpeded. As the last Confederates departed the city, the soldiers stripped bare every garden they passed.

The ruins of the Atlanta Rolling Mill and Hood's supply trains after the munitions were detonated. *Courtesy Library of Congress.*

Other people stayed in Atlanta, however. Confederate Atlantans sought out their Unionist neighbors in hopes of getting some future intercession with the Federal army. Soldiers took the opportunity to desert by hiding among the remaining civilian population. The army had to leave its remaining wounded behind, and the city's Unionists hid Federal soldiers among them, sometimes even dressing them in Confederate uniforms, to save them from transfer to Andersonville Prison by the retreating Southern army. Civilians also joined the soldiers in looting whatever remained.

Due to bureaucratic failure, five locomotives (including the General of the Great Locomotive Chase) with eighty-one boxcars, including twenty-eight cars filled with munitions, had failed to leave Atlanta while the Macon & Western Railroad had remained open. On September 1, 1864, as the last Confederate defenders of the wrecked and robbed city marched south, Hood had the trains set ablaze. His munitions cars exploded with such force that Union soldiers felt the force of the blast in their trenches. Sherman, even twenty miles away in Jonesboro, heard the explosion and saw the glow of the columns of flames. The force of the munitions being set off demolished the adjoining Atlanta Rolling Mill to ground level. (The fires and explosion appear as one of the most memorable scenes in the movie *Gone With the Wind.*) Hood's soldiers continued their evacuation by the firelight of the burning warehouses and exploding ammunition as civilians and deserters looted stores.

On September 2, Mayor James M. Calhoun held an impromptu meeting with some members of the city council and remaining leading citizens at Peachtree and Marietta at Five Points. At length, he decided to lead a delegation to do what no other Atlanta mayor would ever have to do: surrender the city. Calhoun, with a white flag and accompanied by Thomas G.W. Crusselle, William Markham, Thomas Kile, Julius A. Hayden, Robert Webster and others, passed through the ruins left by the bombardment to find General Sherman. At a fort near the wrecked Ponder house, they encountered Captain Henry M. Scott of the Seventieth Illinois Infantry. There, Calhoun wrote a note to Scott's superior, Brigadier General William T. Ward: "Sir: The fortune of War has placed Atlanta in your hands. As mayor of the city I ask protection to non-combatants and private property." The Twentieth Federal Corps then marched into Atlanta. White flags flew from houses, and women came out to greet the blue-clad soldiers with buckets of water. Defiant little boys still whistled "Dixie" and "The Bonnie Blue Flag," but the Federal bands responded by drowning them out with brass renditions of "Yankee Doodle" and the "Battle Hymn of the Republic." Members of Ferguson's Confederate cavalry fired at the Union soldiers. Mayor Calhoun tried to intercede, but the soldiers nearly shot him.

Confederate stragglers remained in Atlanta, but by nightfall the United States flag flew from the city hall and the campaign had concluded. Exact numbers elude scholars, but overall the marching and fighting from Chattanooga to Lovejoy from May to September 1864 cost the Union army 34,514 men and an estimated loss to the Confederates of approximately 35,000. Sherman's three armies only outnumbered their opponents by ratios of three to two and two to one, but Sherman would receive first-rate replacements and reinforcements. Militia, boys, old men, convicts and draft evaders filled only some of the places left by the 12,000 men lost to Hood in just the three major battles fought in the eight days in July. Overall, historian Albert Castel argues that the greatest mistake made by Hood in all of these battles came from asking his officers and soldiers for more than they could give against a foe with every advantage. He also points out, however, that Sherman missed at least six opportunities to destroy his opponent's army. Johnston and then Hood likely had no opportunity to win some Chickamauga-style victory, in any form, that could have turned back the blue-uniformed hordes. Sherman and his Confederate counterparts all failed, respectively, in that they took administrative roles rather than direct supervision of

Demolishing houses in Atlanta damaged in the bombardment. *From* Harper's Weekly.

operations, with the consequence of losing battles and wasting thousands of lives. The government in Richmond, unable to supply its soldiers and civilians adequately throughout the war, did succeed in a massive transfer of most of the prisoners from Andersonville by railroad in anticipation of Atlanta's fall. (Federal forces only reached the prison at the end of the war, after almost all of the prisoners had left for the Union lines.)

V

Occupation and Destruction

General Sherman learned of the surrender of Atlanta while moving against the Confederate army near Lovejoy as what might have been a new assault on Confederate lines petered out. He began reorganizing his forces so that Major General George H. Thomas and his Army of the Cumberland occupied Atlanta, while Major General O.O. Howard's Army of the Tennessee took position in East Point and Major General John M. Schofield's Army of the Ohio occupied Decatur. His cavalry moved to towns along the flanks of his occupation troops. Sherman entered Atlanta without fanfare on September 7, 1864. He established his headquarters at the home of John Neal (today where Atlanta's city hall stands).

Officers moved into the best of the remaining houses, including Mayor Calhoun's home, while their soldiers tore down most of the other wooden buildings to occupy almost all of the empty spaces in the city with their neat rows of shanties. Foraging parties from both armies stripped the area farms of food and, in some instances, plunder. One Federal expedition of 733 wagons netted eleven thousand bushels of corn and all manner of other provisions. Federal horses had grazed on and wrecked Oakland Cemetery. Vandals broke open graves, sometimes only to steal silver coffin plates. Union soldiers placed dead comrades in mausoleums. In Atlanta and elsewhere under Federal occupation, the slaves declared themselves free.

On September 4, 1864, Sherman proclaimed the city a military post. In the same order, he announced that any remaining civilians had to evacuate. Three days later, as he and the last of his troops moved into the captured city

Above: Atlanta in flames. *From* Harper's Weekly.

Right: The Trout House hotel at State Square. Note the shanties built by the Union soldiers. *Courtesy Library of Congress.*

and its environs, the general wrote to Hood proposing to allow the Atlantans choosing to remain in the Confederacy to remove down the Macon & Western by wagon to the whistle stop known as Rough and Ready. From there, the Confederate army would provide transportation for the new refugees—people forced to leave from instead of move to Atlanta. He did not want the responsibility of feeding or protecting civilians. The Confederate general responded that he understood that he had no real choice in the matter. He consented to a ten-day truce for the removal of the noncombatants but protested the removal of people from their homes.

The two opposing generals then began a now famous correspondence on the treatment of Southern civilians by both militaries. Mayor Calhoun and council members Edward E. Rawson and Levi C. Wells also spoke out against the removal. Registrations for the departure began on September 11, however, and continued for ten days. Eventually, 446 families, including 705 adults, 860 children and 79 servants, left for Rough and Ready with 1,651 parcels of furniture and goods.

Historian Albert Castel wrote of the depopulation of the city as the harshest treatment of civilians during the Civil War, with the exception of the removal of pro-Confederate families in Missouri. Sherman, however, had already ordered this same treatment for any household that provided refuge for guerrillas attacking his railroad supply line. Before then, most of Atlanta's Unionists took advantage of Federal generosity to refugee north, although when word began circulating on November 1 that Sherman's troops planned to abandon the city, families came from as far as thirty miles away to obtain transportation north and away from the fighting. Sherman claimed to have seen thousands of Southerners, black and white, doing this since the beginning of the war.

Sherman also offered to exchange what Confederate prisoners he still held for his own men, except for those soldiers who were unhealthy or wounded or whose enlistments had run out. When Hood turned out to have more such prisoners of war than Sherman's remaining two thousand

Civilians preparing to leave Atlanta. *From* Harper's Weekly.

Confederate prisoners of war guarded by Union soldiers in Atlanta. *Courtesy Library of Congress.*

or so Confederates, he offered to also turn over some one thousand civilian workmen he was holding on the grounds that they, too, served the Confederacy and were subject to militia duty. To the last offer, General Hood offered his refusal.

The tragedy of Atlanta continued with musical accompaniment. Federal and Confederate soldiers did what they could to ease the transit south. Colonel William G. Le Duc of the Twentieth Corps protested the removal but did all he could for the Atlantans being removed. He organized a number of concerts at the Athenaeum, which Mayor Calhoun had closed the previous February, with the widow Rebecca S. Welsh singing and sometimes accompanying herself on the piano. She had two children of her own and four of her recently deceased sister's to support. Welsh came up with the idea when he found an old program of an earlier Atlanta concert likely given for support of the military hospitals.

The victorious general received a number of visitors. George N. Barnard, the famous army photographer, came to the city in early September. Beyond his mandate to record Confederate fortifications, he also made unique, historically priceless photographs of Atlanta on the eve of its final destruction. Other guests to the general's headquarters included many of Georgia's most outspoken Unionists and opponents of secession. Among them, former Atlanta mayor William Markham provided names of Confederates he accused of having persecuted Unionists. Sherman subsequently declared as traitors and outlaws Colonel George W. Lee, Colonel Alex M. Wallace, Captain G. Whit Anderson and Lieutenant (Ely Tillinger) Hunnicutt. He ordered their execution on sight. Markham likely neglected to mention his own many profitable contributions to the Confederate war effort and other questionable actions. He and his fellow self-proclaimed Unionists had not suffered anything that merited killing anyone on sight.

Atlanta's city hall/the Fulton County Courthouse during the Federal occupation of Atlanta. *Courtesy Library of Congress.*

Both Sherman and Hood, now free of the problem of Atlanta, set out to conduct the campaigns that they had wanted. The latter marched west from Lovejoy on September 18 and into north Georgia to cut off the supplies to Sherman through the Western & Atlantic. He then crossed northeast Alabama into Tennessee to draw Sherman out of Georgia. The Army of Tennessee finally entrenched outside Nashville, where it remained until destroyed by Major General George H. Thomas's army on December 15–16, 1864. Hood and his soldiers would pass into legend, so much so that the fictional general would become greater, not only in novels, but also in histories, than the real man as represented in what has become, in modern times, an often-published ditty, set to the tune of the "Yellow Rose of Texas," which his men may never have actually sung:

Union soldiers outside of the house formerly used by General Hood as his headquarters. *Courtesy Library of Congress.*

My feet are torn and bloody
My heart is full of woe,
I'm going back to Georgia
To find my Uncle Joe [General Joseph E. Johnston]
You may talk about your Beauregard,
You may sing of Bobby Lee,
But the gallant Hood of Texas
He played Hell in Tennessee

On October 2, Sherman pursued his foe to Alabama before returning to Atlanta two weeks later. The victor of the Atlanta Campaign now persuaded his old partner General Grant to approve a plan to expose what remained of the Confederacy as an empty shell. Wounded, supplies and excess troops went back to Tennessee before Sherman had Atlanta and the Western & Atlantic Railroad wrecked beyond use by the Confederacy. Bridges on the Chattahoochee burned so brightly that the river seemed on fire. Captain Orlando Poe, Sherman's engineer, built a swinging battering ram with a twenty-one-foot iron bar for demolishing brick and stone buildings of military value. Other buildings came down after the soldiers stuffed them with mattresses and other combustibles. Explosives finished the official work of demolition. A Federal band gave one last performance in the Athenaeum, a rendition of "John Brown's Soul Goes Marching On," before that building, too, finally came down. Sherman personally directed the unsuccessful effort to stop the many unplanned and unauthorized fires from burning the remaining homes.

On November 16, 1864, and with sixty-two thousand men, the general abandoned the city he had struggled so hard to take and began his famous March to the Sea and beyond as the Fourteenth Corps band again played "John Brown's Soul Goes Marching On" with the backdrop of huge towers of flame from the burning of what had become America's Troy. Nine days later, Confederate agents failed in an attempt to set New York on fire, in part out of revenge for Atlanta.

Along their great march, heralded in books, paintings and song, Sherman's infamous "bummers" continued their destruction of Southern railroads while plundering mountains of supplies left at various stations waiting for trains that never came due to Confederate bureaucratic incompetence. "Bow ties," heated iron rails bent around the trees by the soldiers, would be visible in many places along their route for years afterward. Sherman's bummers also famously looted any civilian plantations and farms directly in the path of their three columns. Within less than one week, the blue legions marched into

This page: The destruction done to Civil War Atlanta. *Courtesy Library of Congress.*

Sherman's troops destroying railroad track. *Courtesy Library of Congress.*

central Georgia, to the then capital of Georgia in Milledgeville. On December 21, Sherman entered Savannah with his army. The following year, songwriter Henry Clay Work immortalized the great odyssey with "Marching through Georgia," then and since a wildly popular tune that even proved popular among British and Japanese troops in World War II:

Ring the good ol' bugle, boys, we'll sing another song,
Sing it with the spirit that will start the world along,
Sing it as we used to sing it 50,000 strong
While we were marching through Georgia.

Chorus: Hurrah, hurrah, we bring the jubilee!
Hurrah, hurrah, the flag that makes you free!

So we sang the chorus from Atlanta to the sea
While we were marching through Georgia!

How the darkies shouted when they heard the joyful sound!
How the turkeys gobbled which our commissary found!
How the sweet potatoes even started from the ground
*While we were marching through Georgia!—*CHORUS

Yes, and there were Union men who wept with joyful tears
When they saw the honored flag they had not seen for years.
Hardly could they be restrained from breaking forth in cheers
*While we were marching through Georgia!—*CHORUS

"Sherman's dashing Yankee boys will never reach the coast!"
So the saucy rebels said, and 'twas a handsome boast,
Had they not forgot, alas, to reckon with the host
*While we were marching through Georgia!—*CHORUS

So we made a thoroughfare for freedom and her train,
Sixty miles in latitude, 300 to the main.
Treason fled before us, for resistance was in vain
*While we were marching through Georgia!—*CHORUS

At the end of 1864, however, much of the Gate City lay in ruins. "The general who marched to Hell" boasted of Atlanta as only "a thing of the past."

VI

Reborn from Ashes

Atlanta survived the war and grew so quickly afterward that its destruction in late 1864 appears almost as just another of its occasional economic setbacks. It has no place in the argument over whether the New South was just a mutated form of the Old South or something new. Atlanta existed as something on the outside of the traditional South, a city on the edge of the Midwest that had more in common with Chicago, Cincinnati, Dallas and the like—cities of steam and fire.

The same forces of geography, transportation and economics that created the original city quickly rebuilt it. By December 1864, the two armies that had fought so hard for this Atlanta had both evacuated the ruined city. Hardly had the Union army left in mid-November 1864 than people moved into the ruins and abandoned buildings to build a new Atlanta even before the rubble of the old one had cooled. It became a second Confederate occupation, and despite all that had happened, the city's final great moment of the war came from it being almost the last part of the Southern nation.

Some fifty families managed to avoid removal from the city by Sherman's orders, and by December 7, General W.P. Howard reported that another fifty had arrived since the enemy left. Howard witnessed looters loading some 250 wagons with plunder found in houses abandoned by some of Atlanta's wealthiest families. Many of the people now lived in the homes and pillaged the goods of the now absent wartime profiteers who had taken advantage of them throughout the war. Stealing civilian and public property from the ruins became a vast and profitable new business in Atlanta. Some of these

The 1911 Peace Monument at Piedmont Park that commemorates the tour of reconciliation made by Atlanta's Gate City Guard to Boston and other cities in 1879. *Courtesy Atlanta History Center.*

ad hoc entrepreneurs hobbled together pieces of wrecked houses to rent as residences on property they did not own. They even banded together and formed a provisional city government and police force.

A writer for the recently returned *Atlanta Intelligencer* described the city as still viable but silent except for howling dogs. Unlike recent times, the writer wrote of the eerie absence of the sounds of train whistles blowing, animals baying/mooing/crowing and machines whirring. People no longer walked the streets, and abandoned pets were everywhere. Rubble blocked the sidewalks, while hundreds of dead horses and mules lay in the streets.

Atlantans were returning daily. James M. Calhoun walked twenty miles from Jonesboro, the nearest working railhead, carrying an overcoat and a heavy valise. Sallie Clayton came back with her family on a moonlit night. She remembered walking through the dark past "burnt buildings, piles of bricks, rubbish of all sorts, heaps of ashes and clay and odds and ends of almost everything…wells whose covers had been destroyed." J.J. Toon wrote to Howard that "the property of citizens which survived the devouring flames is the exception to the general destruction & demolition intended by our heartless enemies." Visitors noted Atlanta's burned-out business district and used such words as "demoralized," "cheerless," "mean-looking" and "cheap looking" to describe the city and its inhabitants. Rumors circulated that criminals roamed the streets at night murdering visitors and that a scheme existed to lure former slaves to the coast under false promises of jobs in the timber industry before shipping them to Spanish Cuba for sale back into bondage.

Regular government retuned to the city by December 7. Colonel George Washington Lee came to inspect the extensive damage done to the Western & Atlantic Railroad and to get it running to provide relief for poor families in drought-stricken and war-torn north Georgia. Captain Henry P. Farrow of the Nitre and Mining Bureau came to trade provisions to the local people in exchange for the tons of lead, iron and copper that littered the region's many battlefields. Colonel Luther J. Glenn rounded up Atlanta's previously exempt railroad workers, now without jobs, and anyone else who might qualify to serve in a Confederate army that had only days left to exist. He also sought to arrest persons who had helped the enemy during the occupation of Atlanta. City elections on December 7 returned James M. Calhoun as mayor for his fourth and last one-year term. His city treasury, however, held only $1.64. The council's salary committee still proposed a pay scale for the city officials in Confederate money.

If anyone saw the city's destruction as a biblical judgment against its past, however, the entrepreneurial class failed to get that message. More and more of the leading citizens came back as the war continued into its last months. The *Atlanta Intelligencer* correctly noted that the same economic forces that had built the old city less than twenty years earlier would find the millions of dollars needed to rebuild it. Ads in the newspaper even offered slaves for sale. Business boomed on every level as the city ceased to have its assets wasted on the war. Travel writer Sidney Andrews, among others, noted that Atlanta already did more business than Augusta and Macon combined and had 30 percent more commerce after than before the war. Visitors found navigating the piles of building materials and new construction more of a problem than the ruins. The new Atlanta had a serious problem with brick thieves. People gathered the bones of animals killed in the area's numerous battles for sale as fertilizer. By the end of 1865, the city had issued 338 business licenses, and newcomers complained about high prices for any space.

On May 3, 1865, Colonel B.B. Eggleston of the First Ohio Cavalry arrived, and the United States Army took over the city based on the surrender of General Joseph Johnston and his Army of Tennessee on April 26. The Confederate flag came down for the last time. Federal troops maintained order and made arrests; they fed and helped the thousands of Confederate soldiers passing through the city en route to their homes. The Bureau of Refugees, Freedmen and Abandoned Lands (the Freedmen's Bureau) arrived with the army and distributed ninety-five thousand pounds of food the first month. President Andrew Johnson appointed Columbus, Georgia attorney James M. Johnson as provincial governor. He had opposed the war. Other appointments in Georgia included a number of Atlanta Unionists, including Amherst W. Stone as Federal district attorney.

By the end of 1865, the city clearly had found its way back in spectacular ways. The Atlanta Medical College and the post office had reopened. Banks opened for business. The Freedmen's Bureau provided jobs, education and aid for destitute whites and blacks. The following year, the city had all four of its railroads running, reconstituted fire companies, hotels, a new Atlanta Rolling Mill, an opera, schools (black and white), baseball, a lottery to provide education for Confederate orphans and a growing, prosperous African American community.

The occupying Federal soldiers, however, established the McPherson Barracks, named for the major general James M. McPherson killed in the Battle of Atlanta, a few miles south of the city in 1867. They abandoned it in 1881 but reestablished it as today's Fort McPherson in 1889. During the interim, the army had also temporarily established Fort Mitchell somewhere at or near the site and, unofficially, Hancock Barracks, which became Fort McPherson.

Memorials for the now truly lost cause began in Atlanta in 1866 when Mary A. Williams of Columbus, the widow of Colonel C.J. Williams, buried at Oakland, approached the Clayton family about having an annual commemoration every April 26, the anniversary of General Johnston's surrender. A letter to the public from Mrs. Williams followed, and the Atlanta Ladies' Memorial Association, the second memorial association, was formed by April 15. The Claytons and their neighbors took it upon themselves to clear the trash and weeds from the graves of the Confederate dead at Oakland Cemetery. On the first Confederate Memorial Day, Atlanta's stores closed. Federal authorities, however, only allowed a brief service at the cemetery.

This page: Oakland Cemetery includes three thousand burials of Confederate soldiers and fifteen Union dead from the fighting around Atlanta. *Courtesy Gus Welborn.*

Mrs. John M. Johnson, sister of Confederate generals Howell and T.R.R. Cobb, began the successful effort of this organization to remove the war dead from within ten miles of Atlanta to Oakland Cemetery. Many of the disinterred, more often than not unknown, had only a cap and blanket for covering. Major Joseph H. Morgan found enough scarce lumber to create and paint five hundred new wooden grave markers.

The years of radical Reconstruction did nothing to slow Atlanta's progress. Northern entrepreneurs, new and old, such as Hannibal Kimball and William Markham, respectively, drew and invested capital in the city's resurgence. Military commanders of Georgia chose the Gate City for their headquarters, and in 1868, after a series of complex events, a new state constitution finally moved the capital from isolated, rural Milledgeville to Atlanta. That same year, segregated public schools opened for black and white students. The city had a reputation, as archivist Mike Brubaker wrote, of being the place where newspapers came to die. In 1868, however, the city's greatest and longest-running newspaper, the *Constitution*, first went to press. Atlanta also acquired its first public library. In 1869, Atlanta University, chartered in 1867, started the nucleus of its modern complex of four universities.

The 1870 census demonstrated how far Atlanta had come from ruins only five years earlier. Its population had doubled and then almost tripled since 1860 to 21,789. Of that total, 10,231 (45.6 percent) were African American, compared with only 20 percent in 1850 and 1860. The city had become a magnet for former slaves who sought opportunity and refuge from the racial violence of Reconstruction-era rural Georgia. By then, the pre–Civil War dream of a railroad across northeast Georgia to western North Carolina and beyond had become a reality as track was laid to Gainesville and beyond on the Atlanta & Richmond Air Line. When completed, this railroad allowed Atlanta to expand the shipment of its cotton north without having to go through the Southern ports that too often had controlled the city's commerce in the past. The Gate City had Hannibal Ingalls Kimball's Kimball House, the largest hotel in the South. A new waterworks, universities, sidewalks and much more began as investments in a bright future. Even cotton still found a major place in the economy as Atlanta rose in 1880 to become the fourth-largest inland port for receiving the South's great staple.

The year 1874, the ten-year anniversary of the city's destruction, brought back special memories of its Civil War past. At Oakland, the Ladies' Memorial Association erected a monument to the cemetery's Confederate dead—at that time, at sixty-five feet, the tallest structure in the city. That same year, General William Tecumseh Sherman made a two-day visit to Atlanta and received treatment as a celebrity by the city officials. He had won most of the battles in 1864, but the Gate City had spectacularly overcome its destruction. In 1879, General Sherman revisited Atlanta for the third time. Cynics recommended that fire alarms should sound upon his arrival and that Confederate widows should meet him at the train depot. In fact, the prominent Atlantans who welcomed him included former mayor James M. Calhoun and Governor Joseph E. Brown. That same year, in an unrelated gesture, Captain Joseph F. Burke of Atlanta's celebrated Gate City Guard set out on the Atlanta & Charlotte Air Line to eventually travel to Baltimore, Boston, Hartford, New York, Philadelphia and Washington to celebrate the peace and unity since the war. This tour by a former Confederate company from the Atlanta of Civil War fame became a media sensation in the national press. The members even wore blue uniforms and carried a United States flag. (The Peace Monument, erected in Piedmont Park in 1911, commemorates that tour and its sentiment.) That same year, John Bell Hood died of yellow fever in New Orleans, having had great success in his private life that, as with his military career, still ended disastrously.

The rise of Atlanta would continue despite occasional financial setbacks—and more fires—and by 1880, it had become the largest city in Georgia with a population of 37,409. (Today, the population of the metro area exceeds 5,600,000, only some 57 percent of whom are natives of Georgia.) General Sherman died on February 14, 1891, and Joseph E. Johnston passed on the following March 21 from illness contracted from attending Sherman's funeral.

Historian Rebecca Burns wrote of the strange world of race that developed in this entrepreneurial city by 1897, the year that W.E.B. DuBois, the first black graduate of Harvard, assumed his professorship at Atlanta University, the great center of African American intellectualism. The city had, by then, entire black middle-class neighborhoods, such as Brownsville, that lacked for nothing.

Such a reality owed everything to the Civil War. It would have been unimaginable in the 1860 city. Atlanta's viable African American community would lead, in the coming years, in the national struggle for civil rights across the country. DuBois helped to found the NAACP and the *Journal of African American History*, among his many significant accomplishments. The Reverend Adam Daniel Williams, the son of slave Baptist minister Willis Williams, would found a civil rights dynasty in Atlanta that would include A. D. Williams's grandson, Reverend Martin Luther King Jr. In Shermantown,

Auburn Avenue or "Sweet Auburn" became what Atlanta civil rights pioneer John Wesley Dobbs called "the richest Negro street in the world" through the success of such notable black businessmen as Alonzo Herndon and Henry A. Rucker. It also became a center for African American culture, including music, commemorated today with a National Historic District.

The wealthy black and white leadership of Atlanta, however, lived separately in what Burns describes as parallel universes that were more like islands, each beyond the horizon of the other, surrounded by tens of thousands of the poor of both races. Long before the Civil War, many white Georgians had feared competition for land and jobs by freed slaves. From those families, many of their number would first oppose secession, then the war and finally the Confederacy in fear of losing their status in Southern society, losing the war and, by the emancipation of the slaves, losing the only thing of value that the poor Southern white had. They would believe, and later come to deny, that their Confederate ancestors had fought and died to oppose racial equality. In the African American community, the history of slavery remained a part of their present. Attitudes about race thus originated in encounters with the poor rather than the elite of the other race.

Fear and misunderstanding about race proved as toxic in Atlanta as in any other American city. Henry W. Grady, editor of the *Atlanta Constitution*, promoted a vision of a New South that honored its Confederate heroes while embracing a future of transportation, industry and the modern world. He only reflected the new Atlanta—with monuments to its war dead, huge Confederate Memorial Day commemorations at Oakland, separate conventions of veterans of both armies and a Confederate soldiers' home (occupied 1901–45)—beside the New South's symbols of economic development. At the city's 1895 International Cotton States Exposition, he persuaded famed African American education leader Booker T. Washington of the Tuskegee Institute to give the "Atlanta Compromise," a call to his race for black progress in agriculture and industry before achieving equality and integration into white society.

Compromise, however, could only go so far, even in the Atlanta of Henry Grady and W.E.B. DuBois. Atlanta by 1906 had abandoned its past, or was at least trying to overlook it, when it vigorously came back. By then, according to historian Keith Bohannon, such commemorative sites of the war as the Confederate cemetery in Marietta and Fort Walker in Atlanta's Grant Park had become neglected ruins. That same year, even a Federal veterans' organization, the Georgia Division of the Grand Army of the Republic, failed in its effort to have the battlefields surrounding the city preserved as a national park. On September 22, sensationalized newspaper stories about

The Georgia Confederate Soldiers Home. *Courtesy the author.*

alleged sexual assaults on white women by black men led to thousands of white Atlanta men turning out into the street in a riot that cost twenty-five black men their lives, did thousands of dollars in property damage and injured dozens of citizens of the city's African American community. When Governor Asa Candler called out the National Guard, it largely protected white Atlanta neighborhoods from retaliation. On September 25, the leaders of both sides of the city's racial divide finally publicly met to end the violence, the beginnings of the city's questionable reputation for tolerance. The black leaders agreed to work to keep African American Atlantans in line and confined to their neighborhoods while strictly following the apartheid-style Jim Crow laws and ordinances of the time.

The history of racial survivalist attitudes in Atlanta took another of its many peculiar twists in 1913 with the murder of young factory worker Mary Phagan. The two suspects were the Jewish factory manager Leo Frank and the African American janitor. Reviewing the evidence, the all-white male jury convicted Frank and sentenced him to die. Even the United States Supreme Court finally ruled against his appeals. The governor of Georgia accepted a position with the New York law firm that represented the condemned man before he commuted Frank's sentence to life in prison on the day before Frank would have hanged. The governor claimed that he only acted from his concern that Frank might be innocent. The public believed otherwise. A band of Phagan's most prominent neighbors kidnapped Frank from the state prison farm and lynched him near Mary Phagan's home in Marietta in 1915. That event created a national sensation about anti-Semitism that continues to the present. It has also been the subject of books and movies. No jury ever found any reason to investigate, indict or convict the African American janitor of any serious crime.

Anti-Semitism had existed in Civil War Atlanta, but now it could clearly stand by itself as intolerance in the Gate City. Reportedly, half of Georgia's Jews fled the state in response to the outcry against Frank. On October 12, 1958, in reaction to Rabbi Jacob Rothschild's repeated call for racial desegregation, a group of white supremacists calling themselves the Confederate Underground bombed Atlanta's Reform Jewish Temple on Peachtree Street.

During the 1960s civil rights movement and America's centennial of the Civil War, the city's white leadership commemorated its Confederate heritage while working to keep the city's traditional reputation for racial cooperation a reality. The work of men like Mayor Ivan Allen and *Constitution* editor and publisher Ralph McGill (he earned the Pulitzer Prize for his articles exposing hate crimes in Georgia) spared the city from the negative reputation that lingers in so many southern cities.

That spirit of toleration has gone only so far. In recent years, Atlanta's government often quietly bricked and painted over, literally and figuratively, its Civil War past because of the ties to slavery. In 1974, Maynard H. Jackson Jr. became the first African American mayor of Atlanta and of a major southern city. His administration had to confront issues of the city's Confederate heritage many times before, in 1993 and during his third term, Jackson signed an ordinance banning the state flag of Georgia from the city government because it carried a representation of the Confederate battle flag. (Georgia changed its state flag in 2002, although the current flag closely resembles the first national flag of the Confederate government.) Today, ironically, Mayor Jackson lies in historic Oakland, which is usually closed to new burials, rather than Westview, the city's major cemetery for more than a generation. Nearby, thousands of Confederate soldiers also lay buried beside a statue of a dying lion whose battle flag remains engraved in stone.

In modern times, the motto of the city of Atlanta went from the "city too busy to hate" to "the world's next great city." Its boosters proclaimed, each time, that it had more than regional status with a Beatles performance, a visit by the *Mona Lisa*, notorious serial killings, the centennial Olympic Games, an Egyptian pharaoh and the world's largest complete dinosaurs. The fact that, depending on the statistics of any given day, it has the busiest airport on Earth, the fourth-largest concentration of Fortune 500 companies, the fastest-

The Lion of Atlanta monument honors the some three thousand Confederate dead in Oakland Cemetery. T.M. Brady of Canton, Georgia, carved this thirty-thousand-pound block of marble, at the time the largest single block carving in the world. It was dedicated on Confederate Memorial Day, April 26, 1894. It is a short distance from the site, also in Oakland, of the two-story house from which General Hood watched the Battle of Atlanta. *Courtesy Gus Welborn.*

growing metropolitan area in America and the ninth-largest metropolitan area in the country (and the largest in the southeastern United States) does not seem to be enough.

This continuous need for Atlanta to prove itself began long ago when the city tried and failed to become first the state and later the Confederate capital. It did earn from the war the national notoriety of campaign, battle and legendary tale of destruction. The city of Atlanta would, even before the fires of 1864 completely burned out, play its past for what it could while conversely representing itself as a city of the future.

As with the fictional Atlanta in Tom Wolfe's novel *A Man in Full*, the real modern metropolis more profitably believes in its legends and reputation than in answering hard questions about the present. In a final irony, harkening back to Atlanta's Civil War past, Wolfe might have found a better setting for his story of race and uneasy forced cooperation in his native Richmond than in the Gate City of Georgia with its ongoing struggle for reconciliation between the past and future.

VII

What Remains

As with the implication about the Old South in *Gone With the Wind*, more of Atlanta's Civil War past survives on paper than in the physical world. The city's first directory in 1859 included a history of its progress in just those few years since its beginnings. After the war, the Atlanta Pioneer Women's Society, Wallace P. Reed, Wilbur G. Kurtz and the Pioneer Citizens Society saw to it that the experiences of the people who witnessed the Gate City's destruction and rebirth would survive in various writings and publications. Franklin M. Garrett carried on their work in his monumental *Atlanta and Environs* (1952).

The story of this Civil War Ilium, complete with Trojan (i.e. the Roswell) women, continues to draw the interest of writers, good and bad, inspired by this tale of war, destruction and resurrection. They find their task easier for having access to the vast collections of documents, microfilms and artifacts of the Atlanta History Center (ACH), founded as the Atlanta Historical Society in 1926 in an era when physical remains and survivors of the city's wartime experiences could be found everywhere in the Gate City. The ACH's extensive archive has the papers of historians Wilbur Kurtz and Franklin M. Garrett. Its now defunct historical journals continue to supply Atlanta history scholars with the results of valuable research, as does the *Georgia Historical Quarterly*.

Learning the history, as opposed to the fiction, of early Atlanta where it happened requires time, research, patience and compromise. The State of Georgia identified seemingly every military event during the siege of the city with aluminum markers painted to look like corroded bronze between 1952 and 1959. At the Atlanta History Center, the visitor can also tour extensive museums, historic houses and gardens from all periods of the city's past. Its Civil War military artifact collections are among the most extensive in the world, including the famed DuBose Collection.

Other collections still exist on or near their battlefields. In 1906, the Georgia Division of the Grand Army of the Republic lobbied for an Atlanta-area national battlefield park but ultimately failed. In the post–Civil War competition for national battlefield parks, in the Atlanta area, the choice for just one park to commemorate the Atlanta Campaign finally came down to Kennesaw Mountain and Peachtree Creek. The former won, and the Gate City thus avoided Vicksburg's battlefield problems of being literally sealed in by its past. Today, Kennesaw National Battlefield Park, as with Chickamauga National Battlefield Park, tells the story of the war in north Georgia. Ironically, both battlefields are Confederate victories, as are the modern state-owned Resaca and Pickett's Mill Battlefields. Both national parks have extensive museums and battlefield tours.

The General as portrayed at the Great Locomotive Chase Memorial at Kennesaw, Georgia. *Courtesy Gus Welborn.*

Civil War seekers in the area of the Kennesaw National Battlefield Park have much more to see. The ruins of the cotton mills in Roswell stand as a form of memorial of the forced removal of its textile workers to the north in 1864. In the town of Kennesaw, visitors can tour the Southern Museum of Civil War and Locomotive History. It houses a museum of artifacts of life in the Confederate army and the reconstructed locomotive General that survived the Great Locomotive Chase on April 12, 1862, and the explosion of Hood's ammunition train on September 1, 1864. In 1892, the Nashville, Chattanooga & St. Louis Railroad replaced most of the parts on the frame of the locomotive to make it look as it might have when Federal raiders stole it. The engine became a movie character as the subject of Buster Keaton's great comic motion picture *The General* (1927) and a Disney drama, *The Great Locomotive Chase* (1956). The restored engine toured the country for several years as a historical curiosity until, after a long legal dispute between the City of Chattanooga and the State of Georgia, it moved permanently to Kennesaw in 1972. The museum also has the papers of Colonel James Bogle, the great scholar of the Andrews Raid. Across the street, a memorial with panels of paintings by historian Wilbur Kurtz, erected by the City of Kennesaw, tells the story of the Great Locomotive Chase.

Around the museum and memorial stand some pre–Civil War buildings that provide a free bonus to the visitor of a glimpse of something of the small town as it must have been in April 1862. The Great Locomotive Chase began at the nearby Fletcher House Hotel (also known as the Kennesaw House), today's Marietta Museum of History. A room in the museum appears as it might have looked in 1862. General Sherman used the hotel briefly as a headquarters, but it likely survived the war because the owner, Dix Fletcher, was a Unionist, and his son-in-law served as a Federal spy. Marietta also has a national and a Confederate cemetery. (The historic collection of original buildings used to create the fictional 1860s town of Westville near Lumpkin, Georgia, offers another look at life in Civil War Georgia.)

The problem in the "capital of the New South" and "the city too busy to hate" has been promoting its hopes for a future as "the world's next great city" at the expense of losing connections to its past beyond the names on its street signs and a city seal that depicts a phoenix rising from flames. Even the on-site reconstruction of Fort Standing Peachtree and the Zero Mile Post, the terminal point of the Western & Atlantic Railroad that created the city, remain locked up outside of public view. Smoke stains on a wall that reportedly dates from the 1864 fire, or even earlier, disappeared when Underground Atlanta became a mall, prior to Atlanta hosting the centennial

Southern Museum of Civil War and Locomotive History. *Courtesy the author.*

Olympic Games. Historically significant buildings that survived the Civil War and the later fires still stood across Atlanta as late as the 1950s, only to be torn down for new, usually government, construction.

Atlanta's oldest building has come to be the train depot at Underground Atlanta, across from today's state capitol building. It dates from only 1869 and has even lost two stories to fire. Also in Underground Atlanta stands the last of the city's 1855 gaslights, with a marker telling how freedman barber Solomon Luckie suffered a mortal wound from a shell fragment that ricocheted from it when the lamppost stood at Five Points. On December 26, 1919, the United Daughters of the Confederacy dedicated the lamppost in memory of General A.J. West, prominent Confederate veteran, and on December 15, 1939, Atlantans lit it as the Eternal Light of the Confederacy as part of the celebration of the movie *Gone With the Wind.*

The legends and history of Civil War Atlanta achieved a new and greater notoriety with the novel and movie *Gone With the Wind.* The author, fifth-generation Atlantan Margaret "Peggy" Munnerlyn Mitchell, was born on

The lighting of the Eternal Light of the Confederacy during the opening of *Gone With the Wind* in 1939. *Courtesy Special Collections, Georgia State University, Atlanta.*

November 8, 1900. Raised among survivors and tales of the Civil War, she grew up to be a flapper, a reporter for the *Atlanta Journal Constitution Magazine* and Mrs. John Marsh before an injury left her homebound in the apartment that she and her husband affectionately referred to as "the dump." There, from 1926 to 1929, she worked on her then untitled novel about Civil War Atlanta. It still lacked an introduction and two chapters when she reluctantly allowed Harold Latham of Macmillan Press to read most of the finished chapters in 1935. He had toured the South looking for manuscripts for first novels that might achieve something of the success of Georgian Caroline Miller's 1934 Pulitzer Prize–winning *Lamb in His Bosom* (1933). Latham persuaded Mitchell to finish the work for publication, and it came out in May 1936 as the wildly popular *Gone with the Wind* (the "with" in the title was subsequently capitalized). It earned the Pulitzer Prize in 1937. Macmillan had pitched it to movie studios as a project even before its release as a book. The 1939 motion picture *Gone With the Wind*, starring Clark Gable, Vivien Leigh, Leslie Howard and Olivia de Havilland, swept the 1940 Oscars despite 1939 proving to be the greatest year for movies in cinema history.

The grand opening of *Gone With the Wind* at Lowes Grand Theater, Atlanta, December 15, 1939. *Courtesy Hargrett Rare Book and Manuscripts Library, University of Georgia, Athens.*

The destruction of Civil War Atlanta as a representation of the end of the Old South provided the most dramatic moments in both the novel and the motion picture. Scarlett O'Hara, the central character, begins the story as a frivolous antebellum Southern belle, the type of spoiled child of new money mentioned by the real Sallie Clayton in her memoirs. Scarlett subsequently tries to help in the city's hospitals and crosses the vast sea of wounded at the State Square, today's Underground Atlanta, in search of a doctor. As the Confederate army evacuates a burning city and a munitions train threatens to explode, she famously escapes the city with the aid of successful war profiteer Rhett Butler. On the way home to her ruined Tara plantation in Clayton County, she passes through the recent Jonesboro Battlefield. Other losses due to the war force her to become a successful, if ruthless, postwar Atlanta entrepreneur who sacrifices much to survive but retains the hope that somehow she can regain some of the best of her past.

Margaret Mitchell's ancestors, the Philip Fitzgerald family, resemble the fictional O'Hara household in many specifics that likely came from Mitchell's cousin, and the great lost love of the infamous Doc Holliday, Martha Anne Holliday. Mitchell used a great deal of accurate detail, but some of the major events in the story appear questionable in light of historical documentation. The train depot, for example, actually had bunks for its patients, and Confederate officials, by that time in the story, had evacuated most of the wounded so that they would escape the bombardment. A critic of the time claimed that Atlanta's puritanical society prohibited dancing even among slaves, thereby making the grand ball scene unlikely to have happened. However careful a researcher the author tried to be, not she, her historian brother Stephen Mitchell or her friend the artist historian Wilbur Kurtz (hired as a technical advisor on the movie) actually lived through those times. Circumstantial evidence implies that Margaret Mitchell never read or used any of the then unpublished memoirs of Sallie Conley Clayton.

Among the most popular books and movies ever made, the story of *Gone With the Wind* has its basis in politically colored, heroic American nostalgia and in the racism of its times, laid upon details from Margaret Mitchell's family history and the limited published historical studies available in the 1920s. She wrote almost all of the manuscript before the Great Depression, but many of the viewers of the movie (1939) had recent experiences that they could relate to in the film and in their family stories. Ironically, the Nazis banned the book in their occupied lands because of its perceived message of hope to oppressed people. The French Underground resistance, however, used copies of the work to inspire its members. Margaret Mitchell Marsh died as the result of a traffic accident on August 16, 1949. She lies today in her family plot at Oakland Cemetery.

The apartment where Margaret Mitchell wrote most of the Pulitzer Prize–winning novel from which that movie sprang has also been preserved and was opened as a museum at 990 Peachtree Street by the Atlanta History Center. Twice, however, even it nearly fell to arsonists. The remains of the Philip Fitzgerald house and its fictional *Gone With the Wind* counterpart Tara no longer exist. Clayton and Fayette Counties have small public displays of materials relating to the novel and movie. The Marietta Gone With the Wind Museum: Scarlett on the Square in Marietta, Georgia, has the largest public collection of the movie's memorabilia on display. The Hargrett Rare Book and Manuscripts Library at the University of Georgia Libraries in Athens keeps the largest archives of Margaret Mitchell and *Gone With the Wind*, both book and movie.

At Atlanta's Grant Park, visitors see a massive painting well known to Margaret Mitchell and with a Civil War tie to *Gone With the Wind*. This cyclorama played on the notoriety of the history of the Gate City to name the battle it depicts for Atlanta rather than for Decatur, Bald Hill or Leggett's

Battery. Its home, the city's first park and still its fourth largest, began with Lemuel P. Grant, a native of Maine who came to the city in 1849 to build railroads. He donated ten acres for a fairground in 1850 and later another one hundred acres for the park in 1882. Atlanta businessman George Valentine Gress bought a trainload of exotic animals from a circus that had gone bankrupt in 1889. He donated this collection to the city, the beginnings of today's Zoo Atlanta in Grant Park. In 1897, he and Charles Northern also gave the city the cyclorama of the Battle of Atlanta.

This painting has a spectacular heritage. During the nineteenth century, public panoramas became widely popular in Europe and the United States. Such works usually depicted natural scenes, such as the Mississippi River or the Alps, or violent scenes from the Bible and recent events. A forerunner of the motion picture, they would be typically unrolled over a two-hour period with a narration and musical accompaniment. In one of the first of these public shows in the United States, William J. Knight, one of James Andrews's raiders, provided the narrative of the adventure he participated in known as Georgia's Great Locomotive Chase.

The cyclorama of the Battle of Atlanta in Grant Park. *Courtesy the author.*

In late 1800s America, as time increasingly claimed the Civil War veterans, panoramas of their battles began to appear as enormous cycloramas. These circular paintings presented audiences with a 360-degree view that gave the illusion of actually being in the center of the event.

Friedrich Wilhelm Heine and August Lohr of the American Panorama Company in Milwaukee created this work using a team of artists recruited from similar projects in Germany. The company completed the *Battle of Missionary Ridge* as its first project. In the summer of 1885, they came to Atlanta for field studies, accompanied by artist Theodore Davis as an advisor. The latter had supplied *Harper's Weekly* with illustrations during the war and had witnessed the battle from Sherman's headquarters. (Davis appears in the finished painting.) The red clay eroded ground still looked much as it did in July 1864. Atlantans present during the fighting provided details for the artists, who mounted a forty-foot tower built for the project on Moreland Avenue. Even the house where the painters stored their supplies had stood there during the battle. Created in Milwaukee in 1885–86, this greatest of the panoramas, at 42 feet high and 358 feet long, was the world's largest painting until 2004.

Legend credits Senator John A. Logan as commissioning *The Battle of Atlanta*. The former Federal general allegedly intended for this dramatization of his great battle to be part of what became an unsuccessful campaign for the vice presidency of the United States in 1884. The finished work, also called *Logan's Great Battle*, first went on public display in Detroit on February 26, 1887. However. the general had died on December 26, 1886, and likely never saw it. Thanks to an extensive restoration of the painting in the 1980s, in it he and other Union heroes still ride to the rescue as gray regiments, having broken through the blue lines on July 22, 1864, to make a desperate stand. In another section of the cyclorama, Alabama, Mississippi and South Carolina Confederate soldiers of Manigault's brigade fight from behind cotton bales around the never-to-be-finished Troup Hurt plantation house, a symbol of the besieged, defiant, defeated and dying Old South, almost too dramatic in its symbolism. Between the lines of Confederate and Union troops, battery horses leap out in death throes as the Union artillery kill these draft animals to keep the Southern soldiers from removing the guns of the DeGress battery. A Union soldier passes a canteen to his dying Confederate brother. Atlanta, Decatur, Kennesaw Mountain and Stone Mountain appear in the distance. In the foreground, plaster figures give the painting a three-dimensional effect that blends into the scenes of fighting, fields and houses. For generations, visitors have imagined that they have seen their ancestors' faces in the soldiers hurrying into the desperate battle.

A section of the cyclorama of the Battle of Atlanta. Kennesaw Mountain can be seen on the horizon. *Courtesy the author.*

After touring a few northern cities, the cyclorama of the Battle of Atlanta finally went on display in the Gate City on February 22, 1892, replacing the painting *Missionary Ridge* (later destroyed by a tornado in Nashville) at its special Edgewood Avenue theater. Ticket sales to see the cyclorama had been disappointing everywhere, and after several changes in ownership, G.V. Gress and Charles Northern bought it in 1893. They succeeded in persuading the City of Atlanta to build a new home for the painting in Grant Park. Dime admissions, likely increased by the Cotton States Exposition in 1895, raised $12,000 for charity, despite free admissions for Confederate veterans. Gress and Northern finally donated the cyclorama to the city in 1897 on the condition that the painting, damaged by a snowstorm, and its building receive restoration that included a new roof. Finished just in time for a reunion of Confederate veterans on July 22–23, 1897, the thirty-third anniversary of the battle, admission was again free for the old soldiers. In 1921, the City of Atlanta gave the cyclorama a permanent home in a special neoclassical building by John Francis Downing. The almost completely original Texas, the Civil War locomotive that brought to an end the Federal sabotage operation known as the Great Locomotive Chase, also moved into the Cyclorama Building. Clark Gable, Vivien Leigh and Olivia de Havilland visited the painting as part of the opening of *Gone With the Wind* in 1939. In years past, visitors heard Victor Jory's recorded narrative as they viewed the painting. He had been one of the actors in *Gone With the Wind*. Today, a guide gives a revised live narration. The presentation also includes an introductory film on the Atlanta Campaign narrated by actor James Earl Jones.

Fort Walker is also at Grant Park. A redoubt named for General W.H.T. Walker, killed in the Battle of Atlanta, it is all, or almost all, of the remains of the city's once twelve miles of Civil War fortifications. In the late 1800s, veterans and other veterans had photographs made there among its monuments, cannons and caissons. Vandals eventually stole its brass lion monuments and one cannon. The remaining cannons left in the 1980s, and today this earthwork only has an aluminum marker to tell its story.

Other memorials to the Confederacy and to the Civil War in Atlanta remain despite political correctness and attempts to look away from the past. Monuments erected to the city's Civil War past remain in Oakland Cemetery, along with thousands of Confederate dead, and at Piedmont Park. Rhodes Hall, built in 1902–4, is the headquarters of the Georgia Trust for Historic Preservation and has a 1,250-piece German stained-glass memorial called "The Rise and Fall of the Confederacy."

Vivien Leigh, Clark Gable, Olivia de Havilland and Atlanta mayor William B. Hartsfield at the cyclorama during the 1939 grand opening celebration of the movie *Gone With the Wind*. *Courtesy Atlanta History Center.*

Fort Walker as it appeared in the late 1800s. *Courtesy Atlanta History Center.*

Outside of Atlanta, the United Daughters of the Confederacy began a project in 1912 to carve a memorial to the Confederate nation across Stone Mountain. This enormous gray and pink granite surface had no role in the Atlanta Campaign except as one of General Sherman's enumerable observation posts. Gutzon Borglum, famous for his later work on Mount Rushmore, worked on the project, but the carving ended in 1928 due to funding problems. The State of Georgia purchased the mountain for a park in 1958 and funded the completion of the figures of Jefferson Davis, Robert E. Lee and Thomas J. Jackson between 1964 and 1972.

History, however, sometimes becomes just another traded commodity in the ninth-largest metropolitan area in America. The locomotive Texas still chases the General, as it did in the Great Locomotive Chase of 1862, but at Atlanta's Six Flags Over Georgia amusement park. At the nearby Stone Mountain Park, visitors can experience that historical event at a children's putting golf course. Stone Mountain also has a crude reduced-scale replica of Edward A. Vincent's elegant Atlanta train depot, the one destroyed by Sherman's troops in 1864, and a slave plantation designed to accommodate modern tourist sensibilities.

Appendix

Who Destroyed Civil War Atlanta

The modern seal of the city of Atlanta shows a phoenix rising from flames. Family legends tell of seeing the glow on the horizon from the different burnings of Atlanta. Historian Don H. Doyle wrote, "Atlanta felt what Sherman called 'the hand of war' with greater fury than any other southern city—perhaps more than any American city ever."

The Gate City did fall victim to severe damage from the fighting waged by the opposing armies. Two-thirds of the trees in and around Atlanta disappeared during the war. Confederate engineers demolished houses to clear fields of fire and to build palisades for the city's fortifications. The Federal bombardment severely damaged many buildings. Hood ordered warehouses and a large train of railroad cars, many filled with munitions, destroyed on his evacuation of the city. The resulting explosion and fire did severe damage to the nearby buildings.

Sherman's soldiers, during their occupation, also tore down houses to build shanties, and they erected a massive fort on the south side of Atlanta for a garrison of ten thousand men before abandoning the city. Overall, thirty-two hundred houses were lost in Atlanta, as well as another eighteen hundred homes in the surrounding areas, either for military need or as acts of vandalism. Although the Union soldiers found the city amazingly wide open, an attractive city on a hill and in a forest, the Gate City had a bad reputation for fires from even before the Civil War. The demolitions by the Confederate and Federal forces undoubtedly set off many unintended burnings. Vandals

The destruction left in Atlanta. Note the large siege guns in the upper illustration. *From* Harper's Weekly.

also added to the destruction, as did the fact that the occupiers had shipped north all but one of the city's fire engines. Some Federal soldiers, just returned from destroying whole towns in north Georgia, reportedly had no problem continuing their work in Atlanta, especially when drunk. These fires would continue, off and on, until 1866, when the city had the still-flammable walls of the last of the burned-out buildings from the war pulled down.

Much of the city survived, however. Sherman's engineers intended only to demolish buildings of military value. Survivors of the Federal occupation included the city hall/courthouse, the Masonic Hall, the Medical College, five of the churches, the Gate City Hotel, the businesses on Alabama Street and four hundred houses, including many of Atlanta's finest homes. The churches had seen service as hospitals and thus qualified as of military use, but Father Thomas O'Reilly pleaded successfully for saving his Church of the Immaculate Conception, as well as the city hall building, the nearby residences, the Central Presbyterian, the Second Baptist, Trinity Methodist and St. Phillips Episcopal. Dr. P.P. Noel D'Alvigny similarly saved the Atlanta Medical College, as did the local Masons their hall. Overall, about

one-fourth of the city did survive the war, only to completely disappear, over time, to the city's insatiable growth and rebuilding, as well as to the major fires of May 8, 1908, and May 21, 1917. The last buildings in Atlanta that connected the city to its Civil War past came down in the early 1950s, largely unnoticed and unappreciated.

Bibliography

Allen, Frederick. *Atlanta Rising: The Invention of an International City, 1940–1996.* Atlanta, GA: Longstreet Press, 1996.

Bonds, Russell F. *Stealing the General: The Great Locomotive Chase and the First Medal of Honor.* Yardley, PA: Westholme, 2007.

———. *War Like the Thunderbolt: The Battle and Burning of Atlanta.* Yardley, PA: Westholme, 2009.

Bridges, Herb, and Terryl C. Boodman. Gone With the Wind*: The Definitive Illustrated History of the Book, the Movie, and the Legend.* New York: Simon and Schuster, 1989.

Brown, Barry L., and Gordon R. Elwell. *Crossroads of Conflict: A Guide to Civil War Sites in Georgia.* Athens: University of Georgia Press, 2010.

Bryan, Thomas Conn. *Confederate Georgia.* Athens: University of Georgia Press, 1953.

Burns, Rebecca. *Rage in the Gate City: The Story of the 1906 Race Riot of 1906.* Cincinnati, OH: Emmis Books, 2006.

Byrne, Frank J. "Rebellion and Retail: A Tale of Two Merchants in Confederate Atlanta." *Georgia Historical Quarterly* 79 (1995): 30–56.

Carter, Samuel, III. *The Siege of Atlanta, 1864.* New York: Bonanza Books, 1973.

Castel, Albert. *Decision in the West: The Atlanta Campaign of 1864.* Lawrence: University of Kansas Press, 1992.

Clayton, Sarah Conley. *Requiem for a Lost City: Sallie Clayton's Memoirs of Civil War Atlanta and the Old South.* Edited by Robert S. Davis. Macon, GA: Mercer University Press, 1999.

Coffey, David. *John Bell Hood and the Struggle for Atlanta*. Buffalo Gap, TX: State House Press, 1998.

Cohen, Stan, and James G. Bogle. *The General & the Texas: A Pictorial History of the Andrews Raid, April 12, 1862*. Missoula, MO, 1999.

Cooper, Walter G. *Official History of Fulton County*. Atlanta, GA: self-published, 1933.

Cox, Jacob D. *Sherman's Battle for Atlanta*. Cambridge, MA: Da Capo Press, 1994.

Davis, Robert S. "Georgia Cities on the Eve of the Civil War: The Insurance Reports of C.C. Hines." *Atlanta History* 31 (1987): 50–58.

———. "Hysteria and Literature: Atlanta's First Execution and its Legendary Ties to Organized Crime." *Georgia Historical Quarterly* 92 (Fall 2008): 321–39.

———. "White and Black in Blue: The Recruitment of Federal Units in Civil War North Georgia." *Georgia Historical Quarterly* 85 (2001): 348–74.

———. "William A. Fuller, the Western & Atlantic Railroad, and the Other Great Locomotive Chase." *Chattanooga Regional Historical Journal* 10 (July 2007): 71–80.

Davis, Stephen. "'A Very Barbarous Mode of Carrying on War': Sherman's Artillery Bombardment of Atlanta, July 20–August 24, 1864." *Georgia Historical Quarterly* 79 (1995): 57–90.

DeCredico, Mary A. *Patriotism for Profit: Georgia's Urban Entrepreneurs and the Confederate War Effort*. Chapel Hill: University of North Carolina Press, 1990.

Denney, Ken. "Secrets of George Barnard's Photographs of Atlanta in the Year 1864." www.denneymedia.com/atlanta1864/photoset/photoset.htm.

Digital Library of Georgia. "Atlanta Historic Newspapers Archives." http://atlnewspapers.galileo.usg.edu/atlnewspapers/search.

Dormon, James H., Jr. *Theater in the Ante Bellum South, 1815–1861*. Chapel Hill: University of North Carolina Press, 1967.

Doyle, Don H. *New Men, New Cities, New South: Atlanta, Nashville, Charleston, Mobile, 1860–1910*. Chapel Hill: University of North Carolina Press, 1990.

Dyer, Thomas G. *Secret Yankees: The Union Circle in Confederate Atlanta*. Baltimore, MD: Johns Hopkins University Press, 1999.

Ecelbarger, Gary L. *The Day Dixie Died: The Battle of Atlanta*. New York: Thomas Dunne Books, 2010.

Edwards, Anne. *Road to Tara: The Life of Margaret Mitchell*. New Haven, CT: Ticknor & Fields, 1983.

Ellis, Barbara G. *The Moving Appeal: Mr. McClanahan, Mrs. Dill, and the Civil War's Great Newspaper*. Macon, GA: Mercer University Press, 2003.

Evans, David. *Sherman's Horsemen: Union Cavalry Operations in the Atlanta Campaign*. Bloomington: Indiana University Press, 1966.

Garrett, Franklin. *Atlanta and Environs*. 3 vols. New York: Lewis Historical Publishing Company, 1954.

Gibbons, Robert. "Life at the Crossroads of the Confederacy: Atlanta, 1861–1865." *Atlanta Historical Journal* 23, no. 2 (1979): 11–72.

Glatterhaar, Joseph T. *The March to the Sea and Beyond: Sherman's Troops in the Savannah and Carolinas Campaigns*. New York: New York University Press, 1985.

Graham, Paul K. "Edward Arista Vincent: Antebellum Immigrant, Cartographer and Architect." 2010. Unpublished paper in the possession of the author.

Grimm, John W. *The Engine Thief and the Medal of Honor*. N.p., 2008.

Groom, Winston. *Shrouds of Glory, from Atlanta to Nashville: The Last Great Campaign of the Civil War*. New York: The Atlantic Monthly Press, 1995.

Head, Joe F. *The General: The Great Locomotive Dispute*. Cartersville, GA: Bartow History Center, 1990. [Not a book about the dispute over the General but a very good guide to sites related to the Great Locomotive Chase.]

Hitt, Michael D. *Charged with Treason: Ordeal of 400 Mill Workers during Military Operations in Roswell, Georgia, 1864–1865*. Monroe, NY: Library Research Associates, 1992.

Hoehling, A.A. *Last Train from Atlanta*. New York: Bonanza Books, 1958.

Jones, Robert C. *Retracing the Route of Sherman's Atlanta Campaign and the March to the Sea*. Kennesaw, GA: self-published, 2010.

———. *The W&A, the "General," and the Andrews Raid: a Brief History*. Kennesaw, GA: self-published, 2010. [A very good guide to sites related to the Great Locomotive Chase.]

Kennett, Lee. *Marching Through Georgia: The Story of Soldiers and Civilians During Sherman's Campaign*. New York: HarperCollins, 1995.

Knight, Lucian Lamar. *History of Fulton County Georgia*. Atlanta, GA: A.H. Cawston, 1930.

Kurtz, Elma S. "War Diary of Cornelius R. Hanleiter." *Atlanta Historical Bulletin* 14, no. (1969): 9–13.

Kurtz, Wilbur G. *Atlanta and the Old South*. Atlanta, GA: Atlanta Lithograph Company, 1969.

———. *The Atlanta Cyclorama: The Story of the Famed Battle of Atlanta*. Atlanta, GA: City of Atlanta, 1954.

Lane, Mills B. *Times That Prove People's Principles: Civil War in Georgia*. Savannah, GA: Beehive Press, 1993.

Malone, Alberta. *History of the Atlanta Ladies' Memorial Association 1866–1946 Markers and Monuments*. Atlanta, GA, 1946.

Marszalek, John F. *Sherman: A Soldier's Passion for Order*. New York: The Free Press, 1993.

Martin, Harold H. *Atlanta and Environs: A Chronicle of Its People and Events: Years of Change and Challenge, 1940–1976*. Athens: University of Georgia Press, 1987. [One of two, "volume three" of Franklin Garrett's *Atlanta and Environs*.]

McCarley, J. Britt. *The Atlanta Campaign: A Civil War Driving Tour of Atlanta-Area Battlefields*. Atlanta, GA: Cherokee Press, 1989.

Miers, Earl Schenck Miers. *The General Who Marched to Hell: William Tecumseh Sherman and His March to Fame and Infamy*. New York: Alfred A. Knopf, 1951.

Miles, Jim. *To the Sea: A History and Tour Guide of Sherman's March*. Nashville, TN: Rutledge Hill Press, 1989.

Mitchell, Stephens. "Atlanta: The Industrial Heart of the Confederacy." *Atlanta Historical Bulletin* 1, no. 3 (May 1930): 20–27.

O'Briant, Don. *Looking for Tara: The* Gone With the Wind *Guide to Margaret Mitchell's Atlanta*. Atlanta, GA: Longstreet Press, 1994.

Petite, Mary D. *The Women Will Howl: The Union Army Capture of Roswell and New Manchester, Georgia, and the Forced Relocation of Mill Workers*. Jefferson, NC: McFarland & Co., 2008.

Pioneer Citizens' Society of Atlanta. *Pioneer Citizens' History of Atlanta 1833–1902*. Atlanta, GA: Byrd Publishing, 1902.

Reed, Wallace P. *History of Atlanta, Georgia*. Syracuse, NY: D. Mason & Co., 1889.

Richards, Samuel. *Sam Richards's Civil War Diary: A Chronicle of the Atlanta Home Front*. Edited by Wendy Hamand Venet. Athens: University of Georgia Press, 2009.

Richards, William A. "'We Live Under a Constitution': Confederate Martial Law in Atlanta." *Atlanta History* 33 (1989): 25–33.

Russell, James Michael. *Atlanta 1847–1890: City Building in the Old South and the New*. Baton Rouge: Louisiana State University Press, 1989.

Shavin, Norman. *Days in the Life of Atlanta*. Atlanta, GA: Capricorn Corporation, 1987.

———. *Whatever Became of Atlanta?* N.p., n.d.

Shavin, Norman, and Bruce Galphin. *Atlanta: Triumph of a People*. 2nd ed. Atlanta, GA: Capricorn Corporation, 1985.

Sherman, William T. *Memoirs of General T. Sherman*. 1875. Reprint. New York: Da Capo Press, 1984.

Singer, Ralph Benjamin. "Confederate Atlanta." PhD diss., University of Georgia, 1973.

Smith, Gordon B. *History of the Georgia Militia, 1783–1861*. 4 vols. Milledgeville, GA: Boyd Publishing Company, 2001.

Surdam, David G. *Northern Naval Superiority and the Economics of the American Civil War*. Columbia: University of South Carolina Press, 2001.

Vandiver, Frank E. *Ploughshares into Swords: Josiah Gorgas and Confederate Ordnance*. Austin: University of Texas Press, 1952.

Weiman, David F. "The Economic Emancipation of the Non-Slaveholding Class: Upcountry Farmers in the Georgia Cotton Economy." *Journal of Economic History* 45 (March 1985): 71–93.

———. "Urban Growth on the Periphery of the Antebellum Cotton Belt: Atlanta, 1847–1860." *Journal of Economic History* 48 (June 1988): 259–72.

Wilson, Harold S. *Confederate Industry: Manufacturers and Quartermasters in the Civil War*. Jackson: University Press of Mississippi, 2002.

Wooton, Grigsby H., Jr. "New City of the South: Atlanta, 1843–1873." PhD diss., Johns Hopkins University, 1973.

Wortman, Marc. *The Bonfire: The Siege and Burning of Atlanta*. New York: PublicAffairs, 2009.

Index

L

M

N

O

P

U

V

W

Y

About the Author

Robert S. Davis is director of the Family & Regional History Program and senior professor of history at Wallace State College, Hanceville, Alabama. His many publications include *Requiem for a Lost City: Sallie Clayton's Memoirs of Civil War Atlanta* and *Ghosts & Shadows of Andersonville.* His current projects include a biography of Colonel George Washington Lee, the controversial Confederate provost marshal of Civil War Atlanta.

The author at the grave of Sallie Clayton in Atlanta's Oakland Cemetery (left) and reading a cannon barrel at Atlanta's cyclorama (right). *Courtesy Gus Welborn.*

Visit us at
www.historypress.net

With this series of concise books by Civil War scholars, The History Press honors the 150th anniversary of the War Between the States.

You eat war; you hear war; you talk nothing but war; and when you retire to your bed you dream of war. You wake tired of war but the despot has you by the throat, with a thousand bayonets bristling round you, and you must fight or do worse.

–"Atlanta," *Nashville Daily Press & Times*, June 28, 1864

Prior to the Civil War, Atlanta was at the intersection of four rail lines, rendering the Georgia crossroads the fastest-growing city in the Deep South. As the Confederate States formed, Atlanta was a city deeply divided about secession. By the spring of 1863, war had arrived at the doorstep of Atlanta. Join historian Bob Davis as he tells the story of the devastation that befell Atlanta, the Union occupation and how the "Gate City" was reborn from the ashes.

$21.99

ISBN 978-1-59629-763-0
52199
9 781596 297630

The History Press
www.historypress.net

LOST SKI AREAS of Southern California

INGRID P. WICKEN

Foreword by Doug Pfeiffer